Jonathan Dymond

An Inquiry into the Accordancy of War

With the principles of Christianity, and an examination of the philosophical reasoning by which it is defended.

Jonathan Dymond

An Inquiry into the Accordancy of War
With the principles of Christianity, and an examination of the philosophical reasoning by which it is defended.

ISBN/EAN: 9783337234539

Printed in Europe, USA, Canada, Australia, Japan

Cover: Foto ©Andreas Hilbeck / pixelio.de

More available books at **www.hansebooks.com**

AN INQUIRY

INTO

THE ACCORDANCY OF WAR

WITH

THE PRINCIPLES OF CHRISTIANITY,

AND

AN EXAMINATION OF THE PHILOSOPHICAL REASONING BY WHICH IT IS DEFENDED.

WITH

OBSERVATIONS ON SOME OF THE CAUSES OF WAR AND ON SOME OF ITS EFFECTS.

BY JONATHAN DYMOND.

"Contempt, prior to examination, however comfortable to the mind which entertains it, or however natural to great parts, is extremely dangerous; and more apt than almost any other disposition, to produce erroneous judgments both of persons and opinions. PALEY.

NEW-YORK:

STEREOTYPED FOR AND PRINTED BY ORDER OF THE TRUSTEES OF THE RESIDUARY ESTATE OF LINDLEY MURRAY.

NEW YORK:
WILLIAM WOOD & CO., 61 WALKER STREET.
1870.

ADVERTISEMENT.

LINDLEY MURRAY, the Grammarian, and Author of several excellent school and reading books, in his last will, bequeathed certain funds to Trustees in America, his native country, for several benevolent objects, including the gratuitous distribution of "books calculated to promote piety and virtue, and the truth of Christianity."

The Trustees have heretofore had "The Power of Religion on the Mind, in Retirement, Affliction, and at the Approach of Death,"—and also, "Biographical Sketches and Interesting Anecdotes of Persons of Color," stereotyped, and several thousand copies printed and distributed; and they now present to the public the following work, with a belief that it is well calculated to promote the views designated by L Murray.

1847.

CONTENTS.

Preface 7

I.—CAUSES OF WAR.

Original causes—Present multiplicity 9
Want of inquiry—This want not manifested on parallel subjects . . 10
National irritability 12
"Balance of power" 15
Pecuniary interest—Employment for the higher ranks of society . . 16
Ambition—Private purposes of state policy 19
Military glory 20
    Foundation of military glory—Skill—Bravery—Patriotism—Patriotism not a motive to the soldier.
Books—Historians—Poets 27
    Writers who promote war sometimes assert its unlawfulness.

II.—AN INQUIRY, &c.

Palpable ferocity of war 33
Reasonableness of the inquiry 34
Revealed will of God the sole standard of decision . . . 35
Declarations of great men that Christianity prohibits war . . 36
Christianity 37
General character of Christianity 39
Precepts and declarations of Jesus Christ 39
    Arguments that the precepts are figurative only . . 41
Precepts and declarations of the apostles 46
Objections to the advocate of peace from passages of the Christian Scriptures 48
Prophecies of the Old Testament respecting an era of peace . . 54
Early Christians—Their belief—Their practice—Early Christian writers 56
Mosaic institutions 61
Example of men of piety 64
Objections to the advocate of peace from the distinction between the duties of private and public life 65
    Mode of proving the rectitude of this distinction from the absence of a common arbitrator amongst nations . . . 66
    Mode of proving it *on the principles of expediency* . . 67
    Examination of the principles of expediency as applied to war . 68
    —— of the mode of its application 69
Universality of Christian obligation 71

	Page.
Dr. Paley's "*Moral and Political Philosophy*"—Chapter "on War."	
Mode of discusssing the question of its lawfulness	72
This mode inconsistent with the professed principles of the Moral Pilosophy—with the usual practice of the author	73
Inapplicability of the principles proposed by the Moral Philosophy to the purposes of life	75
Dr. Paley's "*Evidences of Christianity*"	76
Inconsistency of its statements with the principles of the Moral Philosophy	78
Argument in favour of war from the excess of male births	79
———*from the lawfulness of coercion on the part of the civil magistrate*	79
Right of self-defence—Mode of maintaining the right from the instincts of nature	82
Attack of an assassin—Principles on which killing an assassin is defended	84
Consequences of these principles	87
Unconditional reliance upon Providence on the subject of defence	89
Safety of this reliance—Evidence by experience in private life— by natural experience	90
General observations	95

III.—EFFECTS OF WAR.

Social consequences	101
Political consequences	102
Opinions of Dr. Johnson	104
Moral consequences	105

UPON THE MILITARY CHARACTER.

Familiarity with human destruction—with plunder	106
Incapacity for regular pursuits—"half-pay"	107
Implicit submission to superiors.	
Its effects on the independence of the mind	109
——— on the moral character	110
Resignation of moral agency	111
Military power despotic	112

UPON THE COMMUNITY.

Peculiar contagiousness of military depravity	115
Animosity of party—Spirit of resentment	117
Privateering—Its peculiar atrocity	118
Mercenaries—Loan of armies	119
Prayers for the success of war	120
The duty of a subject who believes that all war is incompatible with Christianity	122
Conclusion	124

PREFACE.

The object of the following pages is, to give a view of the principal arguments which maintain the indefensibility and impolicy of **war**, and to examine the reasoning which is advanced in its favour.

The author has not found, either in those works which treat exclusively of war, or in those which refer to it as part of a general system, any examination of the question that embraced it in all its bearings. In these pages, therefore, he has attempted, not only to inquire into its accordancy with Christian principles, and to enforce the obligation of these principles, but to discuss those objections to the advocate of peace which are advanced by philosophy, and to examine into the authority of those which are enforced by the power of habit, and by popular opinion.

Perhaps no other apology is necessary for the intrusion of this essay upon the public, than that its subject is, in a very high degree, important. Upon such a subject as the slaughter of mankind, if there be a doubt, however indeterminate, whether Christianity does not prohibit it—if there be a possibility, however remote, that the happiness and security of a nation can be maintained without it, an examination of such possibility or doubt, may reasonably obtain our attention.—The advocate of peace is, however, not obliged to avail himself of such considerations: at least, if the author had not believed that much more than doubt and possibility can be advanced in support of his opinions, this inquiry would not have been offered to the public.

He is far from amusing himself with the expectation of a general assent to the truth of his conclusions. Some will probably dispute the rectitude of the principles of decision, and some will dissent from the legitimacy of their application. Nevertheless, he believes that the number of those whose opinions will accord with his own is increasing, and will yet much more increase; and this belief is sufficiently confident to induce him to publish an essay which will probably be the subject of contempt to some men, and of ridicule to others. But ridicule and contempt are not potent reasoners.

"Christianity can only operate as an alterative. By the mild diffusion of its light and influence, the minds of men are insensibly prepared to perceive and correct the enormities, which folly, or wickedness, or accident have introduced into their public establishments."* It is in the hope of contributing, in a degree however unimportant or remote, to the diffusion of this light and influence, that the following pages have been written.

For the principles of this little volume, or for its conclusions, no one is responsible but the writer: they are unconnected with any society,

---
* Paley's Moral and Political Philosophy.

benevolent or religious. He has not written it for a present occasion, or with any view to the present political state of Europe. A question like this does not concern itself with the quarrels of the day.

It will perhaps be thought by some readers, that there is contained, in the following pages, greater severity of animadversion than becomes an advocate of peace. But, "let it be remembered, that to bestow good names on bad things, is to give them a passport in the world under a delusive disguise."* The writer believes that wars are often supported, because the system itself, and the actions of its agents, are veiled in glittering fictions. He has therefore attempted to exhibit the nature of these fictions and of that which they conceal; and to state, freely and honestly, both what they are not, and what they are. In this attempt it has been difficult—perhaps it has not been possible—to avoid some appearance of severity: but he would beg the reader always to bear in his recollection, that if he speaks with censure of any class of men, he speaks of them only as a class. He is far from giving to such censure an individual application: Such an application would be an outrage of all candour and all justice. If again he speaks of war as *criminal*, he does not attach guilt, necessarily, to the profession of arms. He can suppose that many who engage in the dreadful work of human destruction, may do it without a consciousness of impropriety, or with a belief of its virtue. But truth itself is unalterable: whatever be our conduct, and whatever our opinions, and whether we perceive its principles or not, those principles are immutable; and the illustration of truth, so far as he has the power of discovering it, is the object of the Inquiry which he now offers to the public.

* Knox's Essays, No. 34.

I.

OBSERVATIONS ON THE CAUSES OF WAR.

Felix, qui potuit rerum cognoscere causas.—Virg.

In the attempt to form an accurate estimate of the moral character of human actions and opinions, it is often of importance to inquire how they have been produced. There is always great reason to doubt the rectitude of that, of which the causes and motives are impure; and if, therefore, it should appear from the observations which follow, that some of the motives to war, and of its causes, are inconsistent with reason or with virtue, I would invite the reader to pursue the inquiry that succeeds them, with suspicion, at least, of the rectitude of our ordinary opinions.

There are some customs which have obtained so generally and so long, that what was originally an effect becomes a cause, and what was a cause becomes an effect, until, by the reciprocal influence of each, the custom is continued by circumstances so multiplied and involved, that it is difficult to detect them in all their ramifications, or to determine those to which it is principally to be referred.

What were once the occasions of wars may be easily supposed. Robbery, or the repulsion of robbers, was probably the only motive to hostility, until robbery became refined into ambition, and it was sufficient to produce a war that a chief was not content with the territory of his fathers. But by the gradually increasing complication of society from age to age, and by the multiplication of remote interests and obscure rights, the motives to war have become so numerous and so technical, that ordinary observation often fails to perceive what they are. They are sometimes known only to a cabinet, which is influenced in its decision by reasonings of which a nation knows little, or by feelings of which it knows nothing; so that of those who personally engage in hostilities, there is, perhaps, not often one in ten who can distinctly tell why he is fighting.

This refinement in the motives of war, is no trifling evidence that they are insufficient or bad. When it is considered how tremendous a battle is, how many it hurries in a moment from the world, how much wretchedness and how much guilt it produces, it would surely appear that nothing but *obvious* necessity should induce us to resort to it. But when, instead of a battle, we have a war with many battles, and of course with multiplied suffering and accumulated guilt, the motives to so dreadful a measure ought to be such as to force themselves upon involuntary observation, and to be written, as it were, in the skies. If, then, a large proportion of a people are often without any distinct perception of the reasons why they are slaughtering mankind, it implies, I think, *prima facie* evidence against the adequacy or the justice of the motives to slaughter.

It would not, perhaps, be affectation to say, that of the reasons why we so readily engage in war, one of the principal is, that we do not inquire into the subject. We have been accustomed, from earliest life, to a familiarity with all its " pomp and circumstance;" soldiers have passed us at every step, and battles and victories have been the topic of every one around us. War, therefore, becomes familiarized to all our thoughts, and interwoven with all our associations. We have never inquired whether these things should be: the question does not even suggest itself. We acquiesce in it, as we acquiesce in the rising of the sun, without any other idea than that it is a part of the ordinary process of the world. And how are we to feel disapprobation of a system that we do not examine, and of the nature of which we do not think? **Want** of inquiry has been the means by which long continued practices, whatever has been their enormity, have obtained the general concurrence of the world, and by which they have continued to pollute or degrade it, long after the few who inquire into their nature have discovered them to be bad. It was by **these means that the slave-trade was so long tolerated by this** land of humanity. Men did not *think* of its iniquity. We were induced to think, and we soon abhorred and then abolished it. In the present moral state of the world, therefore, I believe it is the business of him who would perceive pure morality, to question the purity of that which now obtains.

" The vices of another age," says Robertson, " astonish and shock us; the vices of our own become familiar, and excite little horror."—" The influence of any national custom, both on the understanding, on the heart, and how far it may go towards perverting or extinguishing moral principles of the greatest importance, is remarkable. They who [in 1566] had leisure to reflect and to judge, appear to be no more shocked at the crime of assassination, than the persons who committed it in the heat and impetuosity of passion."* Two hundred and fifty years have added something to our morality. We have learnt, at least, to abhor assassination; and I am not afraid to hope that the time will arrive when historians shall think of war what Robertson thinks of murder, and shall endeavor like him, to account for the ferocity and moral blindness of their forefathers. For I do not think the influence of habit in the perversion or extinction of our moral principles, is in any other thing so conspicuous or deplorable, as in the subject before us. They who are shocked at a single murder in the highway, hear with indifference of the murder of a thousand on the field. They whom the idea of a single corpse would thrill with terror, contemplate that of heaps of human carcasses, mangled by human hands, with frigid indifference. If a murder is committed, the narrative is given in the public newspaper, with many expressions of commiseration, with many adjectives of horror, and many hopes that the perpetrator will be detected. In the next paragraph the editor, perhaps, tells us that he has hurried a second edition to the press, in order that he may be the first to glad the public with the intelligence, that in an engagement which has just taken place, *eight hundred and fifty of the enemy were killed.* By war, the natural impulses of the heart seem to be suspended, as if a fiend of blood were privileged to exercise a spell upon our sensibilities, whenever we contemplated his ravages. Amongst all the shocking and all the terrible

---

* History of Scotland.

scenes the world exhibits, the slaughters of war stand preeminent; yet these are the scenes of which the compassionate and the ferocious, the good and the bad, alike talk with complacency or exultation.

England is a land of benevolence, and to human misery she is of all nations, the most prompt in the extension of relief. The immolations of the Hindoos fill us with compassion or horror, and we are zealously laboring to prevent them. The sacrifices of life by our own criminal executions are the subject of our anxious commiseration, and we are strenuously endeavoring to diminish their number. We feel that the life of a Hindoo or a malefactor is a serious thing, and that nothing but imperious necessity should induce us to destroy the one, or to permit the destruction of the other. Yet what are these sacrifices of life in comparison with the sacrifices of war? In the late campaign in Russia, there fell, during one hundred and seventy-three days in succession, an average of two thousand nine hundred men per day. More than five hundred thousand human beings in less than six months! And most of these victims expired with peculiar intensity of suffering. "Thou that teachest another, teachest thou not thyself?" We are carrying our benevolence to the Indies, but what becomes of it in Russia or at Leipsic? We are laboring to save a few lives from the gallows, but where is our solicitude to save them on the field? Life is life, wheresoever it be sacrificed, and has every where equal claims to our regard. I am not now inquiring whether war is right, but whether we do not regard its calamities with an indifference with which we regard no others, and whether that indifference does not make us acquiesce in evils and in miseries which we should otherwise prevent or condemn.

Amongst the immediate causes of the frequency of war, there is one which is, indisputably, irreconcilable in its nature with the principles of our religion. I speak of the critical sense of national pride, and consequent aptitude of offence, and violence of resentment. National irritability is at once a cause of war, and an effect. It disposes us to resent injuries with bloodshed and destruction ; and a war, when it is begun, inflames and perpetuates the passions that produced it. Those who wish a war, endeavour to rouse the spirit of a people by stimulating their passions. They talk of the insults, or the encroachments, or the contempts of the destined enemy, with every artifice of aggravation; they tell us of foreigners who want to trample upon our rights, of rivals who ridicule our power, of foes who will crush, and of tyrants who will enslave us. These men pursue their object, certainly, by efficacious means; they desire a war, and therefore irritate our passions, knowing that when men are angry they are easily persuaded to fight.

In this state of irritability, a nation is continually alive to occasions of offence; and when we seek for offences, we readily find them. A jealous sensibility sees insults and injuries where sober eyes see nothing, and nations thus surround themselves with a sort of artificial tentacula, which they throw wide in quest of irritation, and by which they are stimulated to revenge, by every touch of accident or inadvertency.

He that is easily offended will also easily offend. The man who is always on the alert to discover trespasses on his honour or his rights, never fails to quarrel with his neighbors. Such a person may be dreaded as a torpedo. We may fear, but we shall not love him; and fear without love, easily lapses into enmity. There are, therefore, many feuds and litigations in the life of such a man, that would never have disturbed its quiet, if he had not captiously snarled at the trespasses of accident, and savagely retaliated insignificant injuries. The viper that we chance to molest, we suffer to live if he continue to be quiet; but if he raise himself in menaces of destruction, we knock him on the head.

It is with nations as with men. If, on every offence we fly to arms, and raise the cry of blood, we shall of necessity, provoke exasperation; and if we exasperate a people as petulant and bloody as ourselves, we may probably continue to butcher one another, until we cease only from emptiness of exchequers, or weariness of slaughter. To threaten war, is therefore often equivalent to beginning it. In the present state of men's principles, it is not probable that one nation will observe another levying men, and building ships, and founding cannon, without providing men and ships and cannon themselves; and when both are thus threatening and defying, what is the hope that there will not be a war?

It will scarcely be disputed that we should not kill one another unless we cannot help it. Since war is an enormous evil, some sacrifices are expedient for the sake of peace; and if we consulted our understandings more and our passions less, we should soberly balance the probabilities of mischief, and inquire whether it be not better to endure some evils that we can estimate, than to engage in a conflict of which we can neither calculate the mischief, nor foresee the event; which may probably conduct us from slaughter to disgrace, and which at last is determined, not by justice, but by power. Pride may declaim against these sentiments; but my business is not with *pride*, but with *reason*; and I think reason determines that it would be more wise, and religion that it would be less wicked, to diminish our punctiliousness and irritability. If nations fought only when they could not be at peace, there would be very little fighting in the world. The wars that are waged for "insults to flags," and an endless train of similar motives, are perhaps generally attributable to the irritability of our pride. We are at no pains to appear pacific towards the offender; our remonstrance is a threat; and the nation, which would give satisfaction to an *inquiry*, will give no other answer to a menace than a menace in return. At length we begin to fight, not because we are aggrieved, but because we are angry.

The object of the haughtiness and petulance which one nation uses towards another, is of course to produce some benefit; to awe into compliance with its demands, or into forbearance from aggression. Now it ought to be distinctly shown, that petulance and haughtiness are more efficacious than calmness and moderation; that an address to the passions of a probable enemy is more likely to avert mischief from ourselves, than an address to their reason and their virtue. Nations are composed of men, and of men with human feelings. Whether with individuals or with communities, "a soft answer turneth away wrath." There is, indeed, something in the calmness of reason—in an endeavour to convince rather than to intimidate—in an honest solicitude for friendliness and peace, which obtains, which commands, which extorts forbearance and esteem. This is the privilege of rectitude and truth. It is an inherent quality of their nature; an evidence of their identity with perfect wisdom. I believe, therefore, that even as it concerns our *interests*, moderation and forbearance would be the most politic. And let not our *duties* be forgotten; for forbearance and moderation are duties, absolutely and indispensably imposed upon us by Jesus Christ.

The "balance of power" is a phrase with which we are made sufficiently familiar, as one of the great objects of national policy, that must be attained at whatever cost of treasure or of blood. The support of this balance, therefore, is one of the great purposes of war, and one of the great occasions of its frequency.

It is, perhaps, not idle to remark, that a balance of power amongst nations, is inherently subject to continual interruption. If all the countries of Europe were placed on an equality to-day, they would of necessity become unequal to-morrow. This is the inevitable tendency of human affairs. Thousands of circumstances which sagacity cannot foresee, will continually operate to destroy an equilibrium. Of men, who enter the world with the same possessions and the same prospects, one becomes rich and the other poor; one harangues in the senate, and another labours in a mine; one sacrifices his life to intemperance, and another starves in a garret. How accurately soever we may adjust the strength and consequence of nations to each other, the failure of one harvest, the ravages of one tempest, the ambition of one man, may unequalize them in a moment. It is, therefore, not a trifling argument against this anxious endeavour to attain an equipoise of power, to find that no equipoise can be maintained. When negotiation has followed negotiation, and treaty has been piled upon treaty, and war has succeeded to war, the genius of a Napoleon, or the fate of an armada, nullifies our labors without the possibility of prevention. I do not know how much nations have gained by a balance of power, but it is worth remembrance that some of those countries which have been most solicitous to preserve it, have been most frequently fighting with each other. How many wars has a balance of power prevented, in comparison with the number that have been waged to maintain it?

It is, indeed, deplorable enough that such a balance is to be desired; and that the wickedness and violence of mankind are so great, that nothing can prevent them from destroying one another but an equality of the means of destruction. In such a state of malignity and outrage, it need not be disputed, that, if it could be maintained, an equality of strength is sufficiently desirable; as tigers may be restrained from tearing one another by mutual fear without any want of savageness. It should be remembered, then, that whatever can be said in favour of a balance of power, can be said only because we are wicked; that it derives all its value from our crimes; and that it is wanted only to restrain the outrage of our violence, and to make us contented to growl when we should otherwise fight.

Wars are often promoted from considerations of interest, as well as from passion. The love of gain adds its influence to our other motives to support them, and without other motives, we know that this love is sufficient to give great obliquity to the moral judgment, and to tempt us to many crimes. During a war of ten years, there will always be many whose income depends on its continuance; and a countless host of commissaries, and purveyors, and agents, and mechanics, commend a war, because it fills their pockets. These men have commonly but one question respecting a war, and that is,—whether they get by it. This is the standard of their decision, and this regulates the measure of their support. If money is in prospect, the desolation of a kingdom is of little concern; destruction and slaughter are not to be put in competition with a hundred a year. In truth, it seems to be the system of the conductors of a war, to give to the sources of gain every possible ramification. The more there are who profit by it, the more numerous will be its supporters; and thus the wishes of the cabinet become united with the avarice of the people, and both are gratified in slaughter and devastation.

A support more systematic and powerful is, however, given to war, because it offers to the higher ranks of society, a profession which unites gentility with profit, and which, without the *vulgarity* of trade, maintains or enriches them. It is of little consequence to inquire whether the distinction of vulgarity between the toils of war and the toils of commerce, be fictitious. In the abstract, it is fictitious; but of this species of reputation public opinion holds the *arbitrium, et jus, et norma*—and public opinion is in favour of war.

The army and the navy therefore afford to the middle and higher classes, a most acceptable profession. The profession of arms is like the profession of law or physic—a regular source of employment and profit. Boys are educated for the army, as they are educated for the bar; and parents appear to have no other idea than that war is part of the business of the world. Of *younger sons*, whose fathers do not choose to support them at the expense of the heir, the army and the navy are the common resource. They would not know what to do without them. To many of these, the news of a peace becomes a calamity: principle is not powerful enough to cope with interest: they prefer the desolation of the world to the loss of a coloneley. It is in this manner that much of the rank, the influence, and the wealth of a country become interested in the promotion of wars; and when a custom is promoted by wealth, and influence, and rank, what is the wonder that it should be continued?

Yet it is a dreadful consideration that the destruction of our fellows should become a business by which to live; and that a man can find no other occupation of gain, than that of butchering his neighbours. It is said (if my memory serves me, by Sir Walter Raleigh) " he that taketh up his rest to live by this profession, shall hardly be an honest man."—" Where there is *no obligation to obey,*" " says Lord Clarendon, " it is a wonderful and an unnatural appetite, that disposes men to be soldiers, that they may know how to live; and what reputation soever it may have in politics, it can have none in religion, to say, that the art and conduct of a soldier is not infused by nature, but by study, experience, and observation; and therefore that men are to *learn it :*—when, in truth, *this common argument is made by appetite to excuse, and not by reason to support,* an ill custom."* People do not often become soldiers in order to serve their country, but to serve themselves. An income is commonly the motive to the great, and idleness to the poor. To plead the love of our country is therefore hypocrisy; and let it be remembered that hypocrisy is itself an evidence, and an acknowledgment, that the motive which it would disguise is bad.

By depending upon war for a subsistence, a powerful inducement is given to desire it; and I would submit it to the conscientious part of the profession, that he who desires a war for the sake of its profits, has lost something of his virtue: he has, at least enlisted one of the most influential of human propensities against

* Lord Clarendon's Essays.

it, and when the prospect of gratification is before him—when the question of war is to be decided—it is to be feared that he will suffer the whispers of interest to prevail, and that humanity, and religion, and his conscience will be sacrificed to promote it. But whenever we shall have learnt the nature of pure Christianity, and have imbibed its dispositions, we shall not be willing to avail ourselves of such a horrible source of profit; nor to contribute to the misery, and wickedness, and destruction of mankind, in order to avoid a false and foolish shame.

It is frequently in the power of individual statesmen to involve a people in a war. "Their restraints," says Knox, "in the pursuit of political objects, are not those of morality and religion, but solely reasons of state, and political caution. Plausible words are used, but they are used to hide the deformity of the real principles. Wherever war is deemed desirable in an interested view, a specious pretext never yet remained unfound;"*—and "when they have once said what they think convenient, how untruly soever, they proceed to do what they judge will be profitable, how unjustly soever; and this, men very absurdly and unreasonably would have called *reason of state*, to the discredit of all solid reason, and all rules of probity."† Statesmen have two standards of morality—a social and a political standard. Political morality embraces all crimes; except, indeed, that it has that technical virtue which requires that he who may kill a hundred men with bullets, should not kill one with arsenic. And from this double system of morals it happens, that statesmen who have no restraint to political enormities but political expediency, are sufficiently amiable in private life. But "probity," says Bishop Watson, "is an uniform principle; it cannot be put on in our private closet, and put off in the council-chamber or the senate:" and I fear that he who is wicked as a statesman, if he be good as a man, has some other motive to goodness than its love; that he is decent in private life, because it is not *expedient* that he should be flagitious. It cannot be hoped that he has much restraint from principle. I believe, however, the time will come, when it will be found that God has instituted but one standard of morality, and that to that standard is required the universal conformity, of nations, and of men.

* Knox's Essays. † Lord Clarendon's Essays.

Of the wars of statesmen's ambition, it is not necessary to speak, because no one to whom the world will listen, is willing to defend them. But statesmen have, besides ambition, many purposes of nice policy which make wars convenient; and when they have such purposes, they are cool speculators in blood. They who have many dependants have much patronage, and they who have much patronage have much power. By a war, thousands become dependent on a minister; and if he be disposed, he can often pursue schemes of guilt, and intrench himself in unpunished wickedness, because the war enables him to silence the clamour of opposition by an office, and to secure the suffrages of venality by a bribe. He has therefore many motives to war, in ambition that does not refer to conquest; or, in fear, that extends only to his office or his pocket: and fear or ambition are sometimes more interesting considerations than the happiness and the lives of men. Or perhaps he wants to immortalize his name by a splendid administration; and he thinks no splendour so great as that of conquest and plunder. Cabinets have, in truth, many secret motives of wars of which the people know little. They talk in public of invasions of right, of breaches of treaty, of the support of honour, of the necessity of retaliation, when these motives have no influence on their determination. Some untold purpose of expediency, or the private quarrel of a prince, or the pique or anger of a minister, are often the real motives to a contest, whilst its promoters are loudly talking of the honour or the safety of the country. The motives to war are indeed without end to their number, or their iniquity, or their insignificance. What was the motive of Xerxes in his invasion of Greece?

It is to be feared that the world has sometimes seen the example of a war, begun and prosecuted for the simple purpose of appeasing the clamours of a people by diverting their attention:

> "I well might lodge a fear
> To be again displaced; which, to avoid,
> I cut them off, and had a purpose now
> To lead out many to the Holy Land,
> Lest rest and lying still might make them look
> Too near into my state. Therefore, my Harry,
> Be it thy course to busy giddy minds
> With foreign quarrels; that action hence borne out
> May waste the memory of former days."

When the profligacy of a minister, or the unpopularity of his measures, has excited public discontent, he can perhaps find no other way of escaping the resentment of the people, than by thus making them forget it. He therefore discovers a pretext for denouncing war on some convenient country, in order to divert the indignation of the public from himself to their new made enemies. Such wickedness has existed, and may exist again. Surely it is nearly the climax of possible iniquity. I know not whether the records of human infamy present another crime of such enormous or such abandoned wickedness. A monstrous profligacy or ferocity that must be, which for the sole purpose of individual interest, enters its closet, and coolly fabricates pretences for slaughter; that quietly contrives the exasperation of the public hatred, and then flings the lighted brands of war amongst the devoted and startling people.

The public, therefore, whenever a war is designed, should diligently inquire into the motives of engaging in it. It should be an inquiry that will not be satisfied with idle declamations on indeterminate dangers, and that is not willing to take any thing upon trust. The public should see the danger for themselves; and if they do not see it, should refuse to be led, blindfold, to murder their neighbours. This, we think, is the public duty, as it is certainly the public interest. It implies a forgetfulness of the ends and purposes of government, and of the just degrees and limitations of obedience, to be hurried into so dreadful a measure as a war, without knowing the reason, or asking it. A people have the power of prevention, and they ought to exercise it. Let me not, however, be charged with recommending violence or resistance. The power of preventing war consists in the power of *refusing to take part in it.* This is the mode of opposing political evil, which Christianity permits, and, in truth, requires. And as it is the most Christian method, so, as it respects war, it were certainly the most efficacious; for it is obvious that war cannot be carried on without the co-operation of the people.

But I believe the greatest cause of the popularity of war, and of the facility with which we engage in it, consists in this; that an idea of glory is attached to military exploits, and of honour to the military profession. Something of elevation is supposed to belong to the character of the soldier; whether it be that we involunta rily presume his personal courage; or that he who makes it his business to defend the rest of the community, acquires the superiority of a protector; or that the profession implies an exemption from the laborious and the "meaner" occupations of life. There is something in war, whether phantom or reality, which glitters and allures; and the allurement is powerful, since we see that it induces us to endure hardships and injuries, and expose life to a continual danger. Men do not become soldiers because life is indifferent to them, but because of some extrinsic circumstances which attach to the profession; and some of the most influential of these circumstances are the fame, the spirit, the honour, the glory, which mankind agree to belong to the warrior. The glories of battle, and of those who perish in it, or who return in triumph to their country, are favourite topics of declamation with the historian, the biographer, and the poet. They have told us a thousand times of *dying heroes*, who "resign their lives amidst the joys of conquest, and filled with England's glory, smile in death;" and thus every excitement that eloquence and genius can command is employed to arouse that ambition of fame which can be gratified only at the expense of blood.

There are many ways in which a soldier derives pleasure from his profession. A military officer* when he walks the streets, is an object of *notice;* he is a man of *spirit*, of *honor*, of *gallantry;* wherever he be, he is distinguished from ordinary men; he is an acknowledged *gentleman*. If he engage in battle, he is *brave*, and *noble*, and *magnanimous:* If he be killed, he has *died for his country;* he has *closed his career with glory*. Now all this is agreeable to the mind; it flatters some of its strongest and most pervading passions; and the gratification which these passions derive from war, is one of the great reasons why men so willingly engage in it.

Now we ask the question of a man of reason, what is the foundation of this fame and glory? We profess that, according to the best of our powers of discovery, no solid foundation can be found. Upon the foundation, whatever it be, an immense structure is however raised—a structure so vast, so brilliant, so at-

---

* These observations apply also to the naval profession; but I have in this passage, as in some other parts of the Essay, mentioned only *soldiers*, to prevent circumlocution.

tractive, that the greater portion of mankind are content to gaze in admiration, without any inquiry into its basis, or any solicitude for its durability.—If, however, it should be, that the gorgeous temple will be able to stand only till Christian truth and light become predominant, it surely will be wise of those who seek a niche in its apartments as their paramount and final good, to pause ere they proceed. If they desire a reputation that shall outlive guilt and fiction, let them look to the basis of military fame. If this fame should one day sink into oblivion and contempt, it will not be the first instance in which wide-spread glory has been found to be a glittering bubble, that has burst, and been forgotten. Look at the days of chivalry. Of the ten thousand Quixottes of the middle ages, where is now the honour or the name? Yet poets once sang their praises, and the chronicler of their achievments believed he was recording an everlasting fame. Where are now the glories of the tournament? Glories

"Of which all Europe rung from side to side."

Where is the champion whom princes carassed, and nobles envied? Where are now the triumphs of Duns Scotus, and where are the folios that perpetuated his fame? The glories of war have indeed outlived these. Human passions are less mutable than human follies; but I am willing to avow my conviction that these glories are alike destined to sink into forgetfulness; and that the time is approaching, when the applauses of heroism, and the splendours of conquest, will be remembered only as follies and iniquities that are past. Let him who seeks for fame, other than that which an era of Christian purity will allow, make haste; for every hour that he delays its acquisition, will shorten its duration. This is certain, if there be certainty in the promises of Heaven.

In inquiring into the foundation of military glory, it will be borne in mind, that it is acknowledged by our adversaries, that this glory *is not recognized by Christianity.* No part of the heroic character, says one of the great advocates of war, is the subject of the "commendation, or precepts, or example" of Christ; but the character and dispositions most opposite to the heroic are the subject of them all.* This is a great concession; and it surely

* Dr. Paley.

is the business of Christians, who are sincere in their profession, to doubt the purity of that "glory" and the rectitude of that "heroic character," which it is acknowledged that their Great Instructer never in any shape countenanced, and often obliquely condemned.†

If it be attempted to define *why* glory is allotted to the soldier we suppose that we shall be referred to his skill, or his bravery or his patriotism.

Of *skill* it is not necessary to speak, since very few have the opportunity of displaying it. The business of the great majority is only obedience; and obedience of that sort which almost precludes the exercise of talent.

The rational and immortal being, who raises the edifice of his fame on simple *bravery*, has chosen but on unworthy and a frail foundation. Separate bravery from motives and purposes, and what will remain but that which is possessed by a mastiff or a game-cock? All just, all rational, and we will venture to affirm, all permanent reputation, refers to the mind or to virtue; and what connexion has animal power or animal hardihood with intellect or goodness? I do not decry *courage*. I know that He who was better acquainted than we are with the nature and worth of human actions, attached much value to courage; but he attached none to bravery. Courage He recommended by his precepts, and enforced by his example; bravery He never recommended at all. The wisdom of this distinction, and its accordancy with the principles of his religion, are plain. Bravery requires the existence of many of those dispositions which he disallowed. Animosity, resentment, the desire of retaliation, the disposition to injure and destroy, all this is necessary to bravery; but all this is incompatible with Christianity. The courage which Christianity requires is to bravery what fortitude is to daring—an effort of the mind rather than of the spirits. It is a calm, steady determinateness of purpose, that will not be diverted by solicitation, or awed by fear. "Behold, I go bound in the spirit unto Jerusalem, not knowing the things that shall befall me there, save that the Holy Ghost witnesseth in every city, saying, that bonds and afflictions abide me.

---

† "Christianity quite annihilates the disposition for martial glory."—*Bishop Watson.*

But none of these things move me; neither count I my l fe dear unto myself."* What resemblance has bravery to courage like this? This courage is a virtue, and a virtue which it is difficult to acquire or to practise; and we have, therefore, heedlessly or ingeniously, transferred its praise to another quality, which is inferior in its nature, and easier to acquire, in order that we may obtain the reputation of virtue at a cheap rate. That simple bravery implies much merit, it will be difficult to show—at least, if it be meritorious, we think it will not always be easy, in awarding the honors of a battle, to determine the preponderance of virtue between the soldier and the horse which carries him.

But *patriotism* is the great foundation of the soldier's glory.—Patriotism is the universal theme. To "fight nobly for our country;"—to "fall, covered with glory, in our country's cause;"—to "sacrifice our lives for the liberties, and laws, and religion of our country"—are phrases in the mouth of every man. What do they mean, and to whom do they apply?

We contend that to say generally of those who perish in war, that "they have died for their country," is simply untrue; and for this simple reason, that they did not fight for it. To impugn the notion of ages, is perhaps a hardy task; but we wish to employ, not dogmatism, but argument; and we maintain that men have commonly no such purity of motive, that they have no such patriotism. What is the officer's motive to entering the army? We appeal to himself. Is it not *that he may obtain an income*? And what is the motive of the private? Is it not *that he prefers a life of idleness to industry*, or that he had no wish but *the wish for change*? Having entered the army, what, again, is the soldier's motive to fight? Is it not that fighting is a part of his business—that it is one of the conditions of his servitude? We are not now saying that these motives are bad, but we are saying that they *are* the motives,—and that patriotism is *not*. Of those who fall in battle, is there one in a hundred who even thinks of his country's good? He thinks, perhaps, of its glory, and of the honour of his regiment, but for his country's advantage or welfare, he has no care and no thought. He fights, because fighting is a matter of course to a soldier, or because his personal reputation is at stake, or because

*Acts xx. 22.

ne is compelled to fight, or because he thinks nothing at all of the matter; but seldom, indeed, because he wishes to benefit his country. He fights in battle, as a horse draws in a carriage, because he is compelled to do it, or because he has done it before; but he seldom thinks more of his country's good, than the same horse, if he were carrying corn to a granary, would think he was providing for the comforts of his master.

And, indeed, if the soldier speculated on his country's good, he often cannot tell how it is affected by the quarrel. Nor is it to be expected of him that he should know this. When there is a rumour of a war, there is an endless diversity of opinions as to its expediency, and endless oppositions of conclusion, whether it will tend more to the good of the country, to prosecute or avoid it. If senators and statesmen cannot calculate the good or evil of a war, if one promises advantages and another predicts ruin,—how is the soldier to decide? And without deciding and promoting the good, how is he to be patriotic? Nor will much be gained by saying, that questions of policy form no part of his business, and that he has no other duty than obedience; since this is to reduce his agency to the agency of a machine; and moreover, by this rule, his arms might be directed, indifferently, to the annoyance of another country, or to the oppression of his own. The truth is, that we give to the soldier that of which we are wont to be sufficiently sparing—a *gratuitous* concession of merit. In ordinary life, an individual maintains his individual opinions, and pursues correspondent conduct, with the approbation of one set of men, and the censures of another. One party says, he is benefiting his country, and another maintains that he is ruining it. But the soldier, for whatever he fights, and whether really in promotion of his country's good, or in opposition to it, is always a patriot, and is always secure of his praise. If the war is a national calamity, and was foreseen to be such, still he *fights for his country*. If his judgment has decided against the war, and against its justice or expediency, still he *fights for his country*. He is always virtuous. If he but uses a bayonet, he is always a patriot.

To *sacrifice our lives for the liberties, and laws, and religion of our native land*, are undoubtedly high-sounding words:—but who are they that will do it? Who is it that will sacrifice his life for his country? Will the senator who supports a war? Will the writer who declaims upon patriotism? Will the minister of religion who recommends the sacrifice? Take away glory—take away *war*, and there is not a man of them who will do it. Will you sacrifice your life at *home*? If the loss of your life in London or at York, would procure just so much benefit to your country, as the loss of one soldier in the field, would you be willing to lay your head upon the block? Are you willing to die without notice and without remembrance; and for the sake of this little undiscoverable contribution to your country's good? You would, perhaps, die to *save* your country; but this is not the question. A soldier's death does not save his country. The question is, whether, without any of the circumstances of war, without any of its glory or its pomp, you are willing to resign yourself to the executioner. If you are not, you are not willing to die for your country. And there is not an individual amongst the thousands who declaim upon patriotism, who is willing to do it. He will lay down his life, indeed—but it must be in war: He is willing to die—but it is not for patriotism, but for glory.

The argument we think is clear—that patriotism is NOT the motive; and that in no rational use of language can it be said that the soldier "dies for his country." Men will not sacrifice their lives at all, unless it be in war, and they do not sacrifice them in war from motives of patriotism.*

* We know that there may be, and have been, cases in which the soldier possesses purer motives. An invasion may arouse the national patriotism and arm a people for the unmingled purpose of defending themselves. Here is a definite purpose, a purpose which every individual understands and is interested in: and if he die under such circumstances, we do not deny that his motives are patriotic. The actions to which they prompt, are, however, a separate consideration, and depend for their qualites on the rectitude of war itself. Motives may be patriotic, when actions are bad. I might, perhaps, benefit my country by blowing up a fleet, of which the cargo would injure our commerce. My motive may be patriotic, but my action is vicious.

It is not sufficiently borne in mind, that patriotism, even much purer than this, is not necessarily a virtue. "Christianity," says Bishop Watson, "does not encourage particular patriotism, in opposition to general benignity." And the reason is easy of discovery. Christianity is designed to benefit, not a community, but the world. If it unconditionally encouraged particular patriotism, the duties of a subject of one state would often be in opposition to those of a subject of another. Christianity, however, knows no such inconsistencies; and whatever patriotism therefore, is opposed, in its exercise, to the *general welfare of mankind*, is, in no degree, a virtue.

What then is the foundation of military fame? Is it bravery? Bravery has little connexion with reason, and less with religion. Intellect may despise, and Christianity condemns it. Is it patriotism? Do we refer to the soldier's motives and purposes? If we do, he is not necessarily, or often, a patriot. It was a common expression amongst sailors, and, perhaps, may be so still—"I hate the French, because they are slaves, and wear wooden shoes." This was the sum of their reasonings and their patriotism; and I do not think the mass of those who fight on land, possess a greater.

Crimes should be traced to their causes: and guilt should be fixed upon those who occasion, although they may not perpetrate them. And to whom are the frequency and the crimes of war to be principally attributed? To the directors of public opinion, to the declaimers upon glory:—to men who sit quietly at home in their studies and at their desks; to the historian, and the biographer, and the poet, and the moral philosopher; to the pamphleteer; to the editor of the newspaper; to the teacher of religion. One example of declamation from the pulpit I would offer to the reader:—"Go then, ye defenders of your country; advance, with alacrity, into the field, where God himself musters the hosts to war. Religion is too much interested in your success, not to lend you her aid. She will shed over this enterprise her selectest influence. I cannot but imagine, the virtuous heroes, legislators, and patriots, of every age and country, are bending from their elevated seats to witness this contest, as if they were incapable, till it be brought to a favourable issue, of enjoying their eternal repose. Enjoy that repose, illustrious immortals! Your mantle fell when you ascended, and thousands, inflamed with spirit, and impatient to tread in your steps, are ready to swear by Him that sitteth upon the throne, and liveth for ever and ever, they will protect freedom in her last asylum, and never desert that cause which you sustained by your labours, and cemented with your blood. And thou, sole Ruler among the children of men, to whom the shields of the earth belong,—Gird on thy sword, thou most Mighty. Go forth with our hosts in the day of battle! Impart, in addition to their hereditary valour, that confidence of success which springs from thy presence! Pour into their hearts the spirit of departed heroes! Inspire them with thine own; and while led by thine hand, and fighting under thy banners, open thou their eyes to behold in every valley, and in every plain, what the prophet beheld by the same illumination—chariots of fire and horses of fire. Then shall the strong man be as tow, and the maker of it as a spark; and they shall both burn together, and none shall quench them!"* Of such irreverence of language, employed to convey such violence of sentiment, the world, I hope, has had few examples. Oh! how unlike another exhortation—"Put on mercies, kindness, humbleness of mind, meekness, long-suffering, forbearing one another, and forgiving one another, if any man have a quarrel against any."†

"As long as mankind," says Gibbon, "shall continue to bestow more liberal applause on their destroyers than on their benefactors, the thirst of military glory will ever be the vice of the most exalted characters."‡ "'Tis strange to imagine," says the Earl of Shaftesbury, "that war, which of all things appears the most savage, should be the passion of the most heroic spirits."—But he gives us the reason.—"By a small *misguidance of the affection*, a lover of mankind becomes a ravager; a hero and deliverer becomes an oppressor and destroyer."§ This is the "vice," and this is the "misguidance," which we say, that a large proportion of the writers of every civilized country are continually occasioning

* "The Sentiments proper to the Crisis."—A Sermon, preached October 19, 1803, by Robert Hall, A. M.

† Nor is the preacher inconsistent with *Apostles* alone. He is also inconsistent with himself. In another discourse, delivered in the preceding year, he says :—" The safety of nations *is not to be sought* in ar.s or *in arms. War reverses*, with respect to its objects, *all the rules of morality.* It is nothing less than a temporary *repeal of all the principles of virtue.* It is a system, out of which *almost all the virtues are excluded*, and in which *nearly all the vices are incorporated.* In instructing us to consider *a portion of our fellow creatures as the proper objects of enmity*, it removes, as far as they are concerned, *the basis of all society, of all civilization and virtue;* for the basis of these, is the *good will due to every individual of the species.*" —"Religion," then, we are told, "sheds its selectest influence over that which repeals all the principles of virtue "—over that " in which nearly all the vices are incorporated!" What "religion" it is which does this, I do not know,—but I know that it is not the religion of Christ. TRUTH never led into contradictions like these. Well was it said that we cannot serve two masters. The quotations which we have given, are evidence sufficient that he who *holds with the one neg-lects the other.*

‡ Decline and Fall.

§ Essay on the Freedom of Wit and Humour.

and promoting; and thus, without, perhaps, any purpose of mischief, they constitute more to the destruction of mankind than rapine or ambition. A writer thinks, perhaps, that it is not much harm to applaud bravery. The divergency from virtue may, indeed, be small in its beginning, but the effect of his applauses proceeds in the line of obliquity, until it conducts, at last, to every excess of outrage, to every variety of crime, to every mode of human destruction.

There is one species of declamation on the glories of those who die in battle, to which I would beg the notice of the reader. We are told that when the last breath of exultation and defiance is departed, *the intrepid spirit rises triumphantly from the field of glory to its kindred heavens.* What the hero has been on earth, it matters not: if he dies by a musket ball, he enters heaven in his own right. All men like to suppose that they shall attain felicity at last; and to find that they can attain it without goodness and in spite of vice, is doubtless peculiarly solacing. The history of the hero's achievements wants, indeed, a completeness without it; and this gratuitous transfer of his soul to heaven, forms an agreeable conclusion to his story.

I would be far from "dealing damnation round the land," and undoubtingly believe that of those who fall in battle, many have found an everlasting resting-place. But an indiscriminate consignment of the brave to felicity, is certainly unwarranted; and if wickedness consists in the promotion of wickedness, it is wicked too.

If we say in positive and glowing language, of men indiscriminately, and therefore of the bad, that they *rise on the wings of ecstacy to heaven*, we do all that language can do in the encouragement of profligacy. The terrors of religion *may* still be dreaded; but we have, at least to the utmost of our power, diminished their influence. The mind willingly accepts the assurance, or acquiesces in the falsehood which it wishes to be true; and in spite of all their better knowledge, it may be feared that some continue in profligacy, in the doubting hope that what poets and historians tell them may not be a fiction.

Perhaps the most operative encouragement which these declamations give to the soldier's vices, is contained in this circumstance—that they manifest that public opinion does not hold them in abhorrence. Public opinion is one of the most efficacious regulators of the passions of mankind; and upon the soldier this rein is peculiarly influential. His profession and his personal conduct derive almost all their value and their reputation from the opinion of the world, and from that alone. If, therefore, the public voice does not censure his vices—if, in spite of his vices, it awards him everlasting happiness, what restraint remains upon his passions, or what is the wonder if they be not restrained?

The peculiar application of the subject to our purpose is, however, that these and similar representations are motives to the profession of arms. The military life is made a privileged profession, in which a man may indulge vices with impunity. His occupation is an apology for his crimes, and shields them from punishment. And what greater motive to the military life can be given? Or what can be more atrocious than the crime of those who give it? I know not, indeed, whether the guilt predominates, or the folly. Pitiable imbecility surely it is, that can persuade itself to sacrifice all the beauties of virtue, and all the realities and terrors of religion, to the love of the flowing imagery of *spirits ascending to heaven*. Whether writers shall do this, is a question, not of choice, but of duty: if we would not be the abeters of crime, and the sharers of its guilt, it is imperative that we refrain.

The reader will, perhaps, have observed that some of those writers who are liberal contributors to the military passion, occasionally, in moments when truth and nature seem to have burst the influence of habit, emphatically condemn the system which they have so often contributed to support. There are not many books of which the tendency is more warlike, or which are more likely to stimulate the passion for martial glory, than the Life of Nelson, by Southey; a work, in the composition of which, it probably never suggested itself to the author to inquire whether he were not contributing to the destruction of mankind. A contributor, however, as he has been, we find in another of his works, this extraordinary and memorable passage :—" There is but one community of Christians in the world, and that unhappily, of all communities one of the smallest, enlightened enough to understand the *prohibition of war by our Divine Master*, in its *plain, literal, and undeniable sense;* and conscientious enough to obey it, subduing the very instinct of nature to obedience."* Of these voluntary or involuntary testimonies of the mind against the principles which it habitually possesses, and habitually inculcates, many examples might be given;† and they are valuable testimonies, because they appear to be elicited by the influence of simple nature and unclouded truth. This, I think, is their obvious character. They will commonly be found to have been written when the mind has become sobered by reason, or tranquilized by religion; when the feelings are not excited by external stimulants, and when conquest, and honour, and glory are reduced to that station of importance to which truth assigns them.

But whether such testimonies have much tendency to give conviction to a reader, I know not. Surrounded as they are with a general contrariety of sentiment, it is possible that those who read them may pass them by as the speculations of impracticable morality. I cannot, however, avoid recommending the reader, whenever he meets with passages like these, seriously to examine into their meaning and their force: to inquire whether they be not accordant with the purity of truth, and whether they do not possess the greater authority, because they have forced themselves from the mind when least likely to be deceived, and in opposition to all its habits and all its associations.

Such, then, are amongst the principal of the causes of war. Some consist in want of thought, and some in delusion; some are mercenary, and some simply criminal. Whether any or all of them form a motive to the desolation of empires and to human destruction, such as a good or a reasoning man, who abstracts himself from habitual feelings, can contemplate with approbation, is a question which every one should ask and determine for himself. A conflict of nations is a serious thing: no motive arising from our passions should occasion it, or have any influence in occasioning it: supposing the question of *lawfulness* to be superseded, war should be imposed only by stern, inevitable, unyielding necessity. That such a necessity is contained in these motives, I think cannot be shown. We may, therefore, reasonably question the defensibility of the custom, which is continued by such causes, and supported with such motives. If a tree is

* History of Brazil.   † See "the Inquiry," &c.

known by its fruits, we may also judge the fruit by the tree "Men do not gather grapes of thorns." If the motives to war and its causes are impure, war itself cannot be virtuous; and I would, therefore, solemnly invite the reader to give, to the succeeding Inquiry, his sober and Christian attention.

II.

AN INQUIRY, &c

When I endeavor to divest myself of the influence of habit, and to contemplate a battle with those emotions which it would excite in the mind of a being who had never before heard of human slaughter, I find that I am impressed only with horror and astonishment: and perhaps, of the two emotions, astonishment is the greater. That several thousand persons should meet together, and then deliberately begin to kill one another, appears to the understanding a proceeding so preposterous, so monstrous, that I think a being such as I have supposed, would inevitably conclude that they were mad. Nor, if it were attempted to explain to him some motives to such conduct, do I believe that he would be able to comprehend how any possible circumstances could make it reasonable. The ferocity and prodigious folly of the act would out-balance the weight of every conceivable motive, and he would turn, unsatisfied, away,

"Astonished at the madness of mankind."

There is an advantage in making suppositions such as these; because, when the mind has been familiarized to a practice however monstrous or inhuman, it loses some of its sagacity of moral perception—profligacy becomes honor, and inhumanity becomes spirit. But if the subject is by some circumstance presented to the mind unconnected with any of its previous associations, we see it with a new judgment and new feelings; and wonder, perhaps, that we have not felt so or thought so before. And such occasions it is the part of a wise man to seek; since if they never happen to us, it will often be difficult for us accurately to estimate the qualities of human actions, or to determine whether we approve them from a decision of our judgment, or whether we yield to them only the acquiescence of habit.

It is worthy at least of notice and remembrance, that the only being in the creation of Providence which engages in the wholesale destruction of his own species, is man; that being who alone possesses reason to direct his conduct, who alone is required to love his fellows, and who alone hopes in futurity for repose and peace. All this seems wonderful, and may reasonably humiliate us. The powers which elevate us above the rest of the creation, we have employed in attaining to pre-eminence of outrage and malignity.

It may properly be a subject of wonder, that the arguments which are brought to justify a custom such as war receive so little investigation. It must be a studious ingenuity of mischief, which could devise a practice more calamitous or horrible; and yet it is a practice of which it rarely occurs to us to inquire into the necessity, or to ask whether it cannot be or ought not to be avoided. In one truth, however, all will acquiesce,—that the arguments in favor of such a practice should be unanswerably strong.

Let it not be said that the experience and the practice of other ages have superseded the necessity of inquiry in our own; that there can be no reason to question the lawfulness of that which has been sanctioned by forty centuries; or that he who presumes to question it is amusing himself with schemes of visionary philanthropy. "There is not, it may be," says Lord Clarendon, "a greater obstruction to the investigation of truth, or the improvement of knowledge, than the too frequent appeal, and the too supine resignation of our understanding to antiquity."* Whosoever proposes an alteration of existing institutions will meet, from some men, with a sort of instinctive opposition, which appears to be influenced by no process of reasoning, by no considerations of propriety or principles of rectitude, which defends the existing system because it exists, and which would have equally defended its opposite if that had been the oldest. " Nor is it out of modesty that we have this resignation, or that we do, in truth, think those who have gone before us to be wiser than

---

* Lord Clarendon's Essays.

ourselves; we are as proud and as peevish as any of our progenitors; but it is out of laziness; we will rather take their words than take the pains to examine the reason they govern themselves by."* To those who urge objections from the authority of ages, it is, indeed, a sufficient answer to say that they apply to every long continued custom. Slave-dealers urged them against the friends of the abolition; Papists urged them against Wickliffe and Luther; and the Athenians probably thought it a good objection to an apostle, that "he seemed to be a setter forth of *strange* gods."

It is agreed by all sober moralists, that the foundation of our duty is the will of God, and that his will is to be ascertained by the Revelation which he has made. To Christianity, therefore, we refer in determination of this great question: we admit no other test of truth: and with him who thinks that the decisions of Christianity may be superseded by other considerations, we have no concern; we address not our argument to him, but leave him to find some other and better standard, by which to adjust his principles and regulate his conduct. These observations apply to those objectors who loosely say that "wars are necessary;" for supposing the Christian religion to prohibit war, it is preposterous, and irreverent also, to justify ourselves in supporting it, because "it is necessary." To talk of a divine law which *must be disobeyed*, implies, indeed, such a confusion of moral principles as well as laxity of them, that neither the philosopher nor the Christian are required to notice it. But, perhaps, some of those who say that wars are necessary, do not very accurately inquire what they mean. There are two sorts of necessity—moral and physical; and these, it is probable, some men are accustomed to confound. That there is any physical necessity for war—that people cannot, if they choose, refuse to engage in it, no one will maintain. And a *moral* necessity to perform an action, consists only in the prospect of a certain *degree* of evil by refraining from it. If, then, those who say that "wars are necessary," mean that they are physically necessary, we deny it. If they mean that wars avert greater evils than they occasion, we ask for proof. Proof has never yet been given: and even if we

---

* Lord Clarendon's Essays.

thought that we possessed such proof, we should still be referred to the primary question—"What is the will of God?"

It is some satisfaction to be able to give, on a question of this nature, the testimony of some great minds against the lawfulness of war, opposed as those testimonies are to the general prejudice and the general practice of the world. It has been observed by Beccaria, that "it is the fate of great truths, to glow only like a flash of lightning amidst the dark clouds in which error has enveloped the universe; and if our testimonies are few or transient, it matters not, so that their light be the light of truth." There are, indeed, many, who in describing the horrible particulars of a siege or a battle, indulge in some declamations on the horrors of war, such as has been often repeated and often applauded, and as often forgotten. But such declamations are of little value and of little effect: he who reads the next paragraph finds, probably, that he is invited to follow the path *to glory and to victory—to share the hero's danger and partake the hero's praise;* and he soon discovers that the moralizing parts of his author are the impulse of feelings rather than of principles, and thinks that though it may be very well to write, yet it is better to forget them.

There are, however, testimonies, delivered in the calm of reflection, by acute and enlightened men, which may reasonably be allowed at least so much weight as to free the present inquiry from the charge of being wild or visionary. Christianity indeed needs no such auxiliaries; but if they induce an examination of her duties, a wise man will not wish them to be disregarded.

"They who defend war," says Erasmus, "must defend the dispositions which lead to war; and *these dispositions are absolutely forbidden by the gospel.*—Since the time that Jesus Christ said, "Put up thy sword into its scabbard," *Christians ought not to go to war.*—Christ suffered Peter to fall into an error in this matter, on purpose that, when he had put up Peter's sword, it might remain *no longer a doubt that war was prohibited,* which, before that order, had been considered as allowable."—"I am persuaded," says the Bishop of Llandaff, "*that when the spirit of Christianity shall exert its proper influence* over the minds of individuals, and especially over the minds of public men in their public capacities, over the minds of men constituting the councils of princes, from whence are the issues of peace and war—when this happy period shall arrive, *war will cease throughout the whole Christian world.** "War," says the same acute prelate, "has practices and principles peculiar to itself, *which but ill quadrate with the rule of moral rectitude, and are quite abhorrent from the benignity of Christianity.*† The emphatic declaration which I have already quoted for another purpose, is yet more distinct. *The prohibition of war by our Divine Master, is plain, literal, and undeniable.* ‡ Dr. Vicesimus Knox speaks in language equally specific:— "*Morality and religion forbid war in its motives, conduct, and consequences.*"§

In an inquiry into the decisions of Christianity upon the question of war, we have to refer—to the general tendency of the revelation; to the individual declarations of Jesus Christ: to his practice; to the sentiments and practices of his commissioned followers; to the opinions respecting its lawfulness which were held by their immediate converts; and to some other species of Christian evidence.

It is, perhaps, the capital error of those who have attempted to instruct others in the duties of morality, that they have not been willing to enforce the rules of the Christian Scriptures in their full extent. Almost every moralist pauses somewhere short of the point which they prescribe; and this pause is made at a greater or less distance from the Christian standard, in proportion to the admission, in a greater or less degree, of principles which they have superadded to the principles of the gospel. Few, however, supersede the laws of Christianity, without proposing some principle of "expediency," some doctrine of "natural law," some theory of "intrinsic decency and turpitude," which they lay down as the true standard of moral judgment.—They who reject truth are not likely to escape error. Having mingled with Christianity principles which it never taught, we are not likely to be consistent with truth, or with ourselves; and accordingly, he who seeks for direction from the professed teachers of morality finds his mind bewildered in conflicting theories, and his judgment embarrassed by contradictory instructions. But "wisdom is justified by all her children;" and she is justified, perhaps, by nothing

---

* Life of Bp. Watson.   † Ibid.   ‡ Southey's Hist. of Brazil.   § Essays.

more evidently than by the laws which she has imposed; for *all* who have proposed any standard of rectitude, other than that which Christianity has laid down, or who have admixed any foreign principles with the principles which she teaches, have hitherto proved that they have only been "sporting themselves with their own deceivings."*

It is a remarkable fact that the laws of the Mosaic dispensation, which confessedly was an imperfect system, are laid down clearly and specifically in the form of an express code; whilst those of that purer religion which Jesus Christ introduced into the world, are only to be found, casually and incidentally scattered, as it were, through a volume—intermixed with other subjects—elicited by unconnected events—delivered at distant periods, and for distant purposes, in narratives, in discourses, in conversations, in letters. Into the final purpose of such an ordination (for an ordination it must be supposed to be,) it is not our present business to inquire. One important truth, however, results from the fact as it exists:—that those who would form a general estimate of the moral obligations of Christianity, must derive it, not from *codes*, but from *principles*; not from a multiplicity of directions in what manner we are to act, but from instructions respecting the motives and dispositions by which all actions are to be regulated.†

It appears, therefore, to follow, that in the inquiry whether war is sanctioned by Christianity, a specific declaration of its decision is not likely to be found. If, then, we be asked for a prohibition of war by Jesus Christ, in the express term of a command, in the manner in which *Thou shalt not kill* is directed to murder, we willingly answer that no such prohibition exists:—and it is not necessary to the argument. Even those who would require such a prohibition, are themselves satisfied respecting the obligation of many negative duties, on which there has been no specific deci-

---

* "Even thinking men, bewildered by the various and contradictory systems of moral judgment adopted by different ages and nations, have doubted the existence of any real and permanent standard, and have considered it as the mere creature of habit and education."‡—How has the declaration been verified—"I will destroy the wisdom of the wise!"

† I refer, of course, to those questions of morality which are not specifically decided.

‡ Murray's Inquiries respecting the Progress of Society.

sion in the New Testament. They believe that suicide is not lawful. Yet Christianity never forbade it. It can be shown, indeed, by implication and inference, that suicide could not have been allowed, and with this they are satisfied. Yet there is, probably, in the Christian Scriptures not a twentieth part of as much indirect evidence against the lawfulness of suicide, as there is against the lawfulness of war. To those who require such a command as *Thou shalt not engage in war*, it is therefore, sufficient to reply, that they require that which, upon this and upon many other subjects, Christianity has not chosen to give.

We refer then, first, to the general nature of Christianity, because we think that, if there were no other evidence against the lawfulness of war, we should possess, in that general nature, sufficient proof that it is virtually forbidden.

That the whole character and spirit of our religion are eminently and peculiarly peaceful, and that it is opposed, in all its principles, to carnage and devastation, cannot be disputed.

Have peace one with another. By this shall all men know that ye are my disciples, if ye have love one to another.

Walk with all lowliness and meekness, with long-suffering, forbearing one another in love.

Be ye all of one mind, having compassion one of another; love as brethren, be pitiful, be courteous, not rendering evil for evil, or railing for railing.

Be at peace among yourselves. See that none render evil for evil to any man.—God hath called us to peace.

Follow after love, patience, meekness.—Be gentle, showing all meekness unto all men.—Live in peace.

Lay aside all malice.—Put off anger, wrath, malice.—Let all bitterness, and wrath, and anger, and clamor, and evil speaking be put away from you, with all malice.

Avenge not yourselves.—If thine enemy hunger, feed him; if he thirst, give him drink.—Recompense to no man evil for evil—Overcome evil with good.

Now we ask of any man who looks over these passages, what evidence do they convey respecting the lawfulness of war? Could any approval or allowance of it have been subjoined to these instructions, without obvious and most gross inconsistency? But if war is obviously and most grossly inconsistent with the general character of Christianity—if war could not have been permitted by its teachers, without any egregious violation of their precepts, we think that the evidence of its unlawfulness, *arising from this general character alone*, is as clear, as absolute, and as exclusive as could have been contained in any form of prohibition whatever.

To those solemn, discriminative, and public declarations of Jesus Christ, which are contained in the "sermon on the mount," a reference will necessarily be made upon this great question; and, perhaps, more is to be learnt from these declarations, of the moral duties of his religion, than from any other part of his communications to the world. It should be remarked, in relation to the injunctions which follow, that he repeatedly refers to that less pure and less peaceable system of morality which the law of Moses had inculcated, and contradistinguishes it from his own.

"Ye have heard that it *hath* been said, An eye for an eye, and a tooth for a tooth, but *I* say unto you that ye resist not evil; but whosoever shall smite thee on thy right cheek, turn to him the other also."—"Ye have heard that it *hath* been said, Thou shalt love thy neighbor, and hate thine enemy; but *I* say unto you, Love your enemies; bless them that curse you; do good to them that hate you; and pray for them which despitefully use you and persecute you; for if ye love them only which love you, what reward have ye?"*

There is an extraordinary emphasis in the form of these prohibitions and injunctions. They are not given in an insulated manner. They inculcate the obligations of Christianity as *peculiar* to itself. The previous system of retaliation is introduced for the purpose of prohibiting it, and of distinguishing more clearly and forcibly the pacific nature of the new dispensation.

Of the precepts from the mount, the most obvious characteristic is greater moral excellence and superior purity. They are directed, not so immediately to the external regulation of the conduct, as to the restraint and purification of the affections. In another precept,† it is not enough that an unlawful passion be just so far restrained as to produce no open immorality—the passion itself is forbidden. The tendency of the discourse is to

* Matt. v., &c. † Matt. v. 28.

attach guilt, not to action only, but also to *thought*. "It has been said, Thou shalt not kill, and whosoever shall kill, shall be in danger of the judgment; but *I* say, that whosoever is *angry* with his brother without a cause, shall be in danger of the judgment."* Our lawgiver attaches guilt to some of the violent feelings, such as resentment, hatred, revenge; and by doing this, we contend that he attaches guilt to war. War cannot be carried on without these passions which he prohibits. Our argument, therefore, is syllogistical. War cannot be allowed, if that which is necessary to war is prohibited.

It was sufficient for the law of Moses, that men maintained love towards their neighbours; towards an enemy they were at liberty to indulge rancour and resentment. But Christianity says, "If ye love them only which love you, what reward have ye?— Love your enemies." Now what sort of love does that man bear towards his enemy, who runs him through with a bayonet? We contend that the distinguishing duties of Christianity must be sacrificed when war is carried on. The question is between the abandonment of these duties and the abandonment of war, for both cannot be retained.†

It is, however, objected that the prohibitions, "Resist not evil," &c., are figurative; and that they do not mean that no injury is to be punished, and no outrage to be repelled. It has been asked, with complacent exultation, what would these advocates of peace say to him who struck them on the right cheek? Would they turn to him the other? What would these patient moralists say to him who robbed them of a coat? Would they give him a cloak also? What would these philanthropists say to him who asked them to lend a hundred pounds? Would they not turn away? This is *argumentum ad hominem;* one example amongst the many, of that lowest and most dishonest of all modes of intellectual warfare, which consists in exciting the feelings instead of convincing the understanding. It is, however, some

---

* Matt. v. 22.

† Yet the retention of both has been, unhappily enough, attempted. In a late publication, of which part is devoted to the defence of war, the author gravely recommends soldiers, whilst shooting and stabbing their enemies, to maintain towards them a feeling of "good will."—*Tracts and Essays, by the late William Hey, Esq., F. R. S.*

satisfaction, that the motive to the adoption of this mode of warfare is itself an evidence of a bad cause, for what honest reasoner would produce only a laugh, if he were able to produce conviction? But I must ask, in my turn, what do these objectors say *is* the meaning of the precepts? What *is* the meaning of "resist not evil?" Does it mean to allow bombardment, devastation, murder? If it does not mean to allow all this, it does not mean to allow war. What again do the objectors say is the meaning of "love your enemies," or of "do good to them that hate you?" Does it mean "ruin their commerce"—"sink their fleets"—"plunder their cities"—"shoot through their hearts?" If the precept does not mean all this, it does not mean war. We are, then, not required to define what exceptions Christianity may admit to the application of some of the precepts from the mount; since, whatever exceptions she may allow, it is manifest what she does *not* allow: for if we give to our objectors whatever license of interpretation they may desire, they cannot, either by honesty or dishonesty, so interpret the precepts as to make them allow *war*. I would, however, be far from insinuating that we are left without any means of determining the degree and kind of resistance, which, in some cases, is lawful; although I believe no specification of it can be *previously laid down:* for if the precepts of Christianity had been multiplied a thousand-fold, there would still have arisen many cases of daily occurrence, to which none of them would precisely have applied. Our business, then, *so far as written rules are concerned*, is in all cases to which these rules do not apply, to regulate our conduct by those general principles and dispositions which our religion enjoins. I say, *so far as written rules are concerned;* for "if any man lack wisdom," and these rules do not impart it, "let him ask of God."*

Of the injunctions that are contrasted with "eye for eye, and tooth for tooth," the entire scope and purpose is the suppression of the violent passions, and the inculcation of forbearance, and

---

* It is manifest, from the New Testament, that we are not required to give "a cloak," in every case, to him who robs us of "a coat;" but I think it is equally manifest that we are required to give it not the less because he has robbed us. The circumstance of his having robbed us does not entail an obligation to give; but it also does not impart a permission to withhold. If the necessities of the plunderer require relief, it is the business of the plundered to relieve them

forgiveness, and benevolence, and love. They forbid, not specifically the act, but the spirit of war; and this method of prohibition Christ ordinarily employed. He did not often condemn the individual doctrines or customs of the age, however false or however vicious; but he condemned the passions by which only vice could exist, and inculcated the truth which dismissed every error. And this method was undoubtedly wise. In the gradual alterations of human wickedness, many new species of profligacy might arise which the world had not yet practised. In the gradual vicissitudes of human error, many new fallacies might obtain which the world hath not yet held; and how were these errors and these crimes to be opposed, but by the inculcation of principles that were applicable to every crime and to every error?—principles which tell us not always what is wrong, but which tell us what always is right.

There are two modes of censure or condemnation; the one is to reprobate evil, and the other to enforce the opposite good; and both these modes were adopted by Christ in relation to war. He not only censured the passions that are necessary to war, but inculcated the affections which are most opposed to them. The conduct and dispositions upon which he pronounced his solemn benediction, are exceedingly remarkable. They are these, and in this order: poverty of spirit—mourning—meekness—desire of righteousness—mercy—purity of heart—peace-making—sufferance of persecution. Now let the reader try whether he can propose eight other qualities, to be retained as the general habit of the mind, which shall be more incongruous with war.

Of these benedictions I think the most emphatical is that pronounced upon the *peace-makers:* "Blessed are the peace-makers, for they shall be called the children of God."* Higher praise or a higher title, no man can receive. Now I do not say that these benedictions contain an absolute proof that Christ prohibited war, but I say they make it clear that he did not approve it. He selected a number of subjects for his solemn approbation; and not one of them possesses any congruity with war, and some of them cannot possibly exist in conjunction with it. Can any one believe that he who made this selection, and who distinguished the peace-

* Matt. v. 9.

makers with peculiar approbation, could have sanctioned his followers in murdering one another? Or does any one believe that those who were mourners, and meek, and merciful, and peace-making, could at the same time perpetrate such murder? If I be told that a temporary suspension of Christian dispositions, although necessary to the prosecution of war, does not imply the extinction of Christian principles, or that these dispositions may be the general habit of the mind, and may both precede and follow the acts of war; I answer that this is to grant all that I require, since it grants that when we engage in war, we abandon Christianity.

When the betrayers and murderers of Jesus Christ approached him, his followers asked, "Shall we smite with the sword?" And without waiting for an answer, one of them drew "his sword, and smote the servant of the high-priest, and cut off his right ear."—"Put up thy sword again into its place," said his Divine Master, "for all they that take the sword shall perish with the sword."* There is the greater importance in the circumstances of this command, because it prohibited the destruction of human life in a cause in which there were the best of possible reasons for destroying it. The question, "shall we smite with the sword," obviously refers to the defence of the Redeemer from his assailants by force of arms. His followers were ready to fight for him; and if any reason for fighting could be a good one, they certainly had it. But if, in defence of himself from the hands of bloody ruffians, his religion did not allow the sword to be drawn, for what reason can it be lawful to draw it? The advocates of war are at least bound to show a better reason for destroying mankind, than is contained in this instance in which it was forbidden.

It will, perhaps, be said, that the reason why Christ did not suffer himself to be defended by arms was, that such a defence would have defeated the purpose for which he came into the world, namely, to offer up his life; and that he himself assigns this reason in the context. He does indeed assign it; but the *primary* reason, the *immediate* context, is—"for all they that take the sword shall perish with the sword." The reference to the destined sacrifice of his life is an after-reference. This destined

Matt. xxvi. 51, 52.

sacrifice might, perhaps, have formed a reason why his followers should not fight *then*, but the first, the principal reason which he assigned, was a reason why they should not fight *at all*. Nor is it necessary to define the precise import of the words "for all they that take the sword shall perish with the sword:" since it is sufficient for us all, that they imply reprobation.

To the declaration which was made by Jesus Christ, in the conversation that took place between himself and Pilate, after he had been seized by the Jews, I would peculiarly invite the attention of the reader. The declaration refers specifically to *an armed conflict*, and to *a conflict between numbers*. In allusion to the capability of his followers to have defended his person, he says, "My kingdom is not of this world; if my kingdom were of this world, *then would my servants fight; that I should not be delivered to the Jews:* but now is my kingdom not from hence."* He had before forbidden his "*servants*" to fight in his defence, and now, before Pilate, he assigns the reason for it: "my kingdom is not of this world." This is the very reason which we are urging against war. We say that it is incompatible with his kingdom— with the state which he came into the world to introduce. The incompatibility of war with Christianity is yet more forcibly evinced by the contrast which Christ makes between *his* kingdom and others. It is the ordinary practice in the world for subjects to "fight," and *his* subjects would have fought *if his kingdom had been of this world;* but since it was not of this world,—since its nature was purer and its obligations more pacific,—*therefore* they might not fight.

His declaration referred, not to the act of a single individual who might draw his sword in individual passion, but to an armed engagement between hostile parties; to a conflict for an important object, which one party had previously resolved on attaining, and which the other were ready to have prevented them from attaining, with the sword. It refers, therefore, strictly to a conflict between armed numbers; and to a conflict which, it should be remembered, was in a much better cause than any to which we can now pretend.†

---

* John xviii. 36.

† In the publication to which the note, page 37, refers, the author informs us that the reason why Christ forbade his followers to fight in his defence, was, that it

It is with the apostles as with Christ himself The incessant object of their discourses and writings is the inculcation of peace, of mildness, of placability. It might be supposed that they continually retained in prospect the reward which would attach to 'peace-makers." We ask the advocate of war, whether he discovers in the writings of the apostles, or of the evangelists, any thing that indicates they approved of war. Do the tenor and spirit of their writings bear any congruity with it? Are not their spirit and tenor entirely discordant with it? We are entitled to renew the observation, that the pacific nature of the apostolic writings proves presumptively that the writers disallowed war. That could not be allowed by them, as sanctioned by Christianity, which outraged all the principles that they inculcated.

"Whence come wars and fightings amongst you?" is the interrogation of one of the apostles, to some whom he was reproving for their unchristian conduct. And he answers himself by asking them, "come they not hence, even of your lusts that war in your members?"* This accords precisely with the argument that we urge. Christ forbade the passions which lead to war; and now, when these passions had broken out into actual fighting, his apostle, in condemning war, refers it back to their passions. We have been saying that *the passions are condemned, and, therefore, war;* and now, again, the apostle James thinks, like his Master, that the most effectual way of eradicating war is to eradicate the passions which produce it.

In the following quotation we are told, not only what the arms of the apostles were not, but what they were. "The weapons of our warfare are *not carnal*, but mighty, through God, to be pulling down of strong holds, and bringing into captivity *every thought to the obedience of Christ.*"† I quote this, not only because it assures us that the apostles had nothing to do with military weapons, but because it tells us the object of their warfare—the bringing every *thought* to the obedience of Christ: and this object I would beg the reader to notice, because it accords with the object of Christ

---

would have been to oppose the government of the country. I am glad no better evasion can be found; and this would not have been found, if the author had consulted the reason assigned by the Prohibitor, before he promulgated his own.

* James iv. 1.   † 2 Cor. v. 4.

himself in his precepts from the mount—the reduction of the *thoughts* to obedience. The apostle doubtless knew that, if he could effect this, there was little reason to fear that his converts would slaughter one another. He followed the example of his Master. He attacked wickedness in its root; and inculcated those general principles of purity and forbearance, which, in their prevalence, would abolish war, as they would abolish all other crimes. The teachers of Christianity addressed themselves, not to communities, but men. They enforced the regulation of the passions and the rectification of the heart; and it was probably clear to the perceptions of the apostles, although it is not clear to some species of philosophy, that whatever duties were binding upon one man, were binding upon ten, upon a hundred, and upon the state.

War is not often directly noticed in the writings of the apostles. When it is noticed, it is condemned just in that way in which we should suppose any thing would be condemned, that was *notoriously* opposed to the whole system—just as murder is condemned at the present day. Who can find, in modern books, that murder is formally censured? We may find censures of its motives, of its circumstances, of its degrees of atrocity; but the act itself no one thinks of censuring, because *every one knows* that it is wicked. Setting statutes aside, I doubt whether, if an Otaheitan should choose to argue that Christians allow murder because he cannot find it formally prohibited in their writings, we should not be at a loss to find direct evidence against him. And it arises, perhaps, from the same causes, that a formal prohibition of war is not to be found in the writings of the apostles. I do not believe they *imagined* that Christianity would ever be charged with allowing it. They write as if the idea of such a charge never occurred to them. They did, nevertheless, virtually forbid it; unless any one shall say that they disallowed the passions which occasion war, but did not disallow war itself; that Christianity prohibits the cause, but permits the effect; which is much the same as to say that a law which forbade the administering of arsenic, did not forbid poisoning.—And this sort of reasoning, strange and illogical as it is, we shall by and by find has been gravely adopted against us.

But although the general tenor of Christianity, and many of its direct precepts, appear to me to condemn and disallow war, it is certain that different conclusions have been formed; and many, who are undoubtedly desirous of performing the duties of Christianity, have failed to perceive that war is unlawful to them.

In examining the arguments by which war is defended, two important considerations should be borne in mind—first, that those who urge them, are not simply defending war, they are also defending *themselves*. If war be wrong, their conduct is wrong, and the desire of self justification prompts them to give importance to whatever arguments they can advance in its favour. Their decisions may therefore, with reason, be regarded as in some degree the decisions of a party in the cause. The other consideration is, that the defenders of war come to the discussion prepossessed in its favour. They are attached to it by their earliest habits. They do not examine the question as a philosopher would examine it, to whom the subject was new. Their opinions had been already formed. They are discussing a question which they had already determined. And every man, who is acquainted with the effects of evidence on the mind, knows that under these circumstances, a very slender argument in favour of the previous opinions possesses more influence than many great ones against it. Now all this cannot be predicated of the advocates of peace; they are *opposing* the influence of habit—they are contending *against* the general prejudice—they are, perhaps, dismissing their own previous opinions. And I would submit it to the candour of the reader, that these circumstances ought to attach in his mind, *suspicion* to the validity of the arguments against us.

The narrative of the centurion who came to Jesus at Capernaum, to solicit him to heal his servant, furnishes one of these arguments. It is said that Christ found no fault with the centurion's profession; that if he had disallowed the military character, he would have taken this opportunity of censuring it; and that, instead of such censure, he highly commended the officer, and said of him, "I have not found so great faith, no, not in Israel."*

An obvious weakness in this argument is this; that it is founded, not upon approval, but upon silence. Approbation is

* Matt. viii. 10.

indeed expressed, but it is directed, not to his arms, but to his faith; and those who will read the narrative will find that no occasion was given for noticing his profession. He came to Christ, not as a military officer, but simply as a deserving man. A censure of his profession *might*, undoubtedly, have been pronounced, but it would have been a gratuitous censure, a censure that did not naturally arise out of the case. The objection is in its greatest weight presumptive only, for none can be supposed to countenance every thing that he does not condemn. To observe *silence** in such cases, was, indeed, the ordinary practice of Christ. He very seldom interfered with the civil and political institutions of the world. In these institutions there was sufficient wickedness around him, but some of them, flagitious as they were, he never, on any occasion, even noticed. His mode of condemning and extirpating political vices was by the inculcation of general rules of purity, which, in their eventual and universal application, would reform them all.

But how happens it that Christ did not notice the centurion's religion? He surely was an idolater. And is there not as good reason for maintaining that Christ approved idolatry, because he did not condemn it, as that he approved war because he did not condemn it? Reasoning from analogy, we should conclude that idolatry was likely to have been noticed rather than war; and it is therefore peculiarly and singularly unapt to bring forward the silence respecting war as an evidence of its lawfulness.

A similar argument is advanced from the case of Cornelius, to whom Peter was sent from Joppa; of which it is said, that although the gospel was imparted to Cornelius by the especial direction of Heaven, yet we do not find that he therefore quitted his profession, or that it was considered inconsistent with his new character. The objection applies to this argument as to the last, that it is built upon silence, that it is simply negative. *We do not find* that he quitted the service:—I might answer, Neither do we find that he continued in it. We only know nothing of the matter: and the evidence is therefore so much less than proof, as silence is less than approbation. Yet, that the account is silent respecting any disapprobation of war, might have been a

---

* See a future quotation from the "Moral and Political Philosophy."

reasonable ground of argument under different circumstances. It might have been a reasonable ground of argument, if the primary object of Christianity had been the reformation of political institutions, or, perhaps, even if her primary object had been the regulation of the external conduct; but her *primary* object was neither of these. She directed herself to the reformation of the heart, knowing that all other reformation would follow. She embraced indeed both morality and policy, and has reformed or will reform both—not so much immediately as consequently; not so much by filtering the current, as by purifying the spring. The silence of Peter, therefore, in the case of Cornelius, will serve the cause of war but little; that little is diminished when urged against the positive evidence of commands and prohibitions, and it is reduced to nothingness, when it is opposed to the *universal tendency* and *object* of the revelation.

It has sometimes been urged that Christ paid taxes to the Roman government at a time when it was engaged in war, and when, therefore, the money that he paid would be employed in its prosecution. This we shall readily grant; but it appears to be forgotten by our opponents, that, if this proves war to be lawful, they are proving too much. These taxes were thrown into the exchequer of the state, and a part of the money was applied to purposes of a most iniquitous and shocking nature; sometimes probably to the gratification of the emperor's personal vices and to his gladiatorial exhibitions, &c., and certainly to the support of a miserable idolatry. If, therefore, the payment of taxes to such a government proves an approbation of war, it proves an approbation of many other enormities. Moreover, the argument goes too far in relation even to war; for it must necessarily make Christ approve of all the Roman wars, without distinction of their justice or injustice—of the most ambitious, the most atrocious, and the most aggressive; and these even our objectors will not defend. The payment of tribute by our Lord was accordant with his usual system of avoiding to interfere in the civil or political institutions of the world.

"Let him that has no sword sell his garment, and buy one."[*] This is another passage that is brought against us. "For what

---

[*] Luke xxii. 36.

purpose," it is asked, were they to buy swords, if swords might not be used?" I doubt whether with some of those who advanced this objection, it is not an objection of words rather than of opinion. I doubt whether they themselves think there is any weight in it. To those, however, who may be influenced by it, I would observe, that, as it appears to me, a sufficient answer to the objection may be found in the immediate context :—" Lord, behold here are two swords," said they; and he immediately answered. " It is enough." How could two be enough when eleven were to be supplied with them? That swords, in the sense and for the purpose of military weapons, were even intended in this passage, there appears much reason for doubting. This reason will be discovered by examining and connecting such expressions as these: "The Son of man is not come to destroy men's lives, but to save them," said our Lord. Yet, on another occasion, he says, " I came not to send peace on earth, but a *sword.*" How are we to explain the meaning of the latter declaration? Obviously by understanding "sword" to mean something far other than steel. For myself, I see little reason for supposing that physical weapons were intended in the instruction of Christ. I believe they were not intended, partly because no one can imagine his apostles were in the habit of using such arms, partly because they declared that the weapons of their warfare were *not* carnal, and partly because the word "*sword*" is often used to imply "dissension," or the religious warfare of the Christian. Such a use of language is found in the last quotation; and it is found also in such expressions as these; "*shield* of faith"—"*helmet* of salvation"—"*sword* of the Spirit"— "I have *fought* the good *fight* of faith."

Put it will be said that the apostles did provide themselves with swords, for that on the same evening they asked, "shall we smite with the sword?" This is true, and I think it may probably be true also, that some of them provided themselves with swords in *consequence* of the injunction of their Master. But what then? The reader of the New Testament will find that hitherto the destined teachers of Christianity were very imperfectly acquainted with the nature of their Master's religion—their conceptions of it were yet gross and Jewish. The very question that is brought against us, and the succeeding conduct of Peter, evince how little they yet knew that *His kingdom was not of this world, and that his* *servants might not fight.* Even after the resurrection, they seemed to be still expecting that his purpose was to establish a temporal government, by the inquiry—" Lord, wilt thou at this time restore again the kingdom unto Israel?"* Why do we avail ourselves of the conduct of the apostles, before they themselves knew the duties of Christianity? Why, if this example of Peter be authority to us, do we not approve the *subsequent* example of this same apostle, in denying his Master?

Why, indeed, do we urge the conduct of Peter at all, when that conduct was immediately condemned by Christ? And, had it not been condemned, how happens it, that if he allowed his followers the use of arms, he healed the only wound which we find they ever inflicted with them?

It appears to me, that the apostles acted on this occasion upon the principles on which they had wished to act on another, when they asked, " Shall we command fire to come down from heaven to consume them?" And that their Master's principles of action were also the same in both—" Ye know not what manner of spirit ye are of; for the Son of man is not come to destroy men's lives, but to save them." *This* is the language of Christianity; and I would seriously invite him who now justifies "destroying men's lives," to consider what manner of spirit he is of.

I think, then, that no argument arising from the instruction to buy swords can be maintained. This, at least, we know, that when the apostles were *completely* commissioned, they neither used nor possessed them. An extraordinary imagination he must have, who conceives of an apostle, preaching peace and reconciliation, crying, "forgive injuries"—"love your enemies"—"render not evil for evil;" and at the conclusion of the discourse, if he chanced to meet with violence or insult, promptly drawing his sword, and maiming or murdering the offender. We insist upon this consideration. If swords were to be worn, swords were to be used; and there is no rational way in which they could have been used, but some such as that which we have been supposing. If, therefore, the words, " Let him that has no sword sell his garment, and buy one," do not mean to authorize *such a use* of the sword, they do not mean to authorize its use at all: And those

---

* Acts i. 6.

who adduce the passage must allow its application in such a sense, or they must exclude it from any application to their purpose.

It has been said, again, that when soldiers came to John the Baptist to inquire of him what they should do, he did not direct them to leave the service, but to be content with their wages. This, also, is at best but a negative evidence. It does not prove that the military profession was wrong, and it certainly does not prove that it was right. But in truth, if it asserted the latter, Christians have, as I conceive, nothing to do with it; for I think that we need not inquire what John allowed, or what he forbade. He, confessedly, belonged to that system which required "an eye for an eye, and a tooth for a tooth;" and the observations which we shall by-and-by make on the authority of the law of Moses, apply, therefore, to that of John the Baptist. Although it could be proved (which it cannot be) that he allowed wars, he acted not inconsistently with his own dispensation; and with that dispensation we have no business. Yet, if any one still insists upon the authority of John, I would refer him for an answer to Jesus Christ himself. What authority *He* attached to John on questions relating to his own dispensation, may be learned from this—" The *least* in the kingdom of heaven is *greater* than he."

Such are the arguments which are adduced from the Christian Scriptures, by the advocates of war. Of these arguments, those derived from the cases of the centurion and of Cornelius, are simply negative. It is not pretended that they possess *proof*. Their strength consists in silence, and of this silence there appears to be sufficient explanation. Of the objection arising from the payment of tribute, I know not who will avail himself. It is nullified by itself. A nearly similar observation applies to the instruction to *buy swords;* and with the case of John the Baptist I do not conceive that we have any concern. In these five passages, the sum of the New Testament evidences in favour of war unquestionably consists: they are the passages which men of acute minds, studiously seeking for evidence, have selected. And what are they? There is not one of them, except the payment of tribute and the instruction to buy swords, of which it is even said by our opponents that it *proves* any thing in favour of war. A

"NOT" always intervenes—the centurion was *not* found fault with: Cornelius was *not* told to leave the profession: John did *not* tell the soldiers to abandon the army. I cannot forbear to solicit the reader to compare these objections with the pacific evidence of the gospel which has been laid before him; I would rather say to compare it with the gospel itself; for the sum, the tendency of the *whole revelation* is in our favour.

In an inquiry whether Christianity allows of war, there is a subject that always appears to me to be of peculiar importance—the prophecies of the Old Testament respecting the arrival of a period of universal peace. The belief is perhaps general among Christians, that a time will come when vice shall be eradicated from the world, when the violent passions of mankind shall be repressed, and when the pure benignity of Christianity shall be universally diffused. That such a period will come we indeed know assuredly, for God has promised it.

Of the many prophecies of the Old Testament respecting it, I will refer only to a few from the writings of Isaiah. In his predictions respecting the "last times," by which it is not disputed that he referred to the prevalence of the Christian religion, the prophet says,—" They shall beat their swords into ploughshares, and their spears into pruning-hooks; nation shall not lift the sword against nation, neither shall they learn war any more."* Again, referring to the same period, he says,—" They shall not hurt nor destroy in all my holy mountain, for the knowledge of the Lord shall cover the earth as the waters cover the sea."† And again, respecting the same era,—" Violence shall be no more heard in thy land, wasting nor destruction within thy borders."‡

Two things are to be observed in relation to these prophecies: first, that it is the will of God that war should eventually be abolished. This consideration is of importance, for if war be not accordant with His will, war cannot be accordant with Christianity, which is the revelation of His will. My business, however, is principally with the second consideration—*that Christianity will be the means of introducing this period of peace.* From those who say that our religion sanctions war, an answer must be expected to questions such as these :—By what instrumentality and by the

---

* Isaiah ii. 4. † Ibid. xi. 9. ‡ Ibid. lx. 18.

diffusion of what principles, will the prophecies of Isaiah be fulfilled? Are we to expect some new system of religion, by which the imperfections of Christianity shall be removed, and its deficiencies supplied? Are we to believe that God sent his only Son into the world to institute a religion such as this—a religion that, in a few centuries, would require to be altered and amended? If Christianity allows of war, they must tell us what it is that is to extirpate war. If she allows "violence, and wasting, and destruction," they must tell us what are the principles that are to produce gentleness, and benevolence, and forbearance.—I know not what answer such inquiries will receive from the advocate of war, but I know that Isaiah says the change will be effected by *Christianity:* And if any one still chooses to expect another and a purer system, an apostle may perhaps repress his hopes:—" If we, or an angel from heaven," says Paul, " preach any other gospel than that which *we* have preached unto you, let him be accursed."*

Whatever the principles of Christianity will require hereafter, they require now. Christianity, *with its present principles and obligations,* is to produce universal peace. It becomes, therefore, an absurdity, a simple contradiction, to maintain that the principles of Christianity allow of war, when they, and they only, are to eradicate it. If we have no other guarantee of peace than the existence of our religion, and no other hope of peace than in its diffusion, how can that religion sanction war? The conclusion that it does not sanction it appears strictly logical: I do not perceive that a demonstration from Euclid can be clearer; and I think that if we possessed no other evidence of the unlawfulness of war, there is contained in this a proof which prejudice cannot deny, and which sophistry cannot evade.

The case is clear. A more perfect obedience to that same gospel which we are told sanctions slaughter, will be the means, and the only means, of exterminating slaughter from the world. It is not from an alteration of Christianity, but from an assimilation of Christians to its nature, that we are to hope. It is because we violate the principles of our religion, because we are not what they require us to be, that wars are continued. If we will not be

* Gal. i. 8.

peaceable, let us then, at least, be honest, and acknowledge that we continue to slaughter one another, not because Christianity permits it, but because we reject her laws.

The Christian ought to be satisfied, on questions connected with his duties, by the simple rules of his religion. If those rules disallow war, he should inquire no farther; but since I am willing to give conviction to the reader by whatever means, and since truth carries its evidence with greater force from accumulated testimony, I would refer to two or three other subjects in illustration of our principles, or in confirmation of their truth.

The opinions of the earliest professors of Christianity upon the lawfulness of war are of importance; because they who lived nearest to the time of its Founder were the most likely to be informed of his intentions and his will, and to practise them without those adulterations which we know have been introduced by the lapse of ages.

During a considerable period after the death of Christ, it is certain, then, that his followers believed he had forbidden war, and that, in consequence of this belief, many of them refused to engage in it; whatever were the consequences, whether reproach, or imprisonment, or death. These facts are indisputable: "It is as easy," says a learned writer of the seventeenth century, "to obscure the sun at mid-day, as to deny that the primitive Christians renounced all revenge and war." Of all the Christian writers of the second century, there is not one who notices the subject, who does not hold it to be unlawful for a Christian to bear arms; "and," says Clarkson, "it was not till Christianity became corrupted, that Christians became soldiers."*

Our Saviour inculcated mildness and peaceableness; we have seen that the apostles imbibed his spirit, and followed his example; and the early Christians pursued the example and imbibed the spirit of both. "This sacred principle, this earnest recommendation of forbearance, lenity, and forgiveness, mixes with all the writings of that age. There are more quotations in the apostolical fathers, of texts which relate to these points than of any

---

* "Essays on the Doctrines and Practice of the Early Christians as they relate to War." To this Essay I am indebted for much information on the present part of our subject.

other. Christ's sayings had struck them. *Not rendering*, says Polycarp the disciple of John, *evil for evil, or railing for railing, or striking for striking, or cursing for cursing.*† Christ and his apostles delivered general precepts for the regulation of our conduct. It was necessary for their successors to apply them to their practice in life. And to what did they apply the pacific precepts which had been delivered? They applied them to war: they were assured that the precepts absolutely forbade it. This belief they derived from those very precepts on which we have insisted: They referred expressly to the same passages in the New Testament, *and from the authority and obligation of those passages*, they refused to bear arms. A few examples from their history will show with what undoubting confidence they believed in the unlawfulness of war, and how much they were willing to suffer in the cause of peace.

Maximilian, as it is related in the Acts of Ruinart, was brought before the tribunal to be enrolled as a soldier. On the proconsul's asking his name, Maximilian replied, "I am a Christian, and cannot fight." It was, however, ordered that he should be enrolled, but he refused to serve, still alleging *that he was a Christian*. He was immediately told that there was no alternative between bearing arms and being put to death. But his fidelity was not to be shaken,—"I cannot fight," said he, "if I die." The proconsul asked who had persuaded him to this conduct; "My own mind," said the Christian, "and He who has called me." It was once more attempted to shake his resolution by appealing to his youth and to the glory of the profession, but in vain;—"I cannot fight," said he, "for any earthly consideration." He continued steadfast to his principles, sentence was pronounced upon him, and he was led to execution.

The primitive Christians not only refused to be enlisted in the army, but when they embraced Christianity whilst already enlisted, they abandoned the profession at whatever cost. Marcellus was a centurion in the legion called Trajana. Whilst holding this commission he became a Christian, and believing, in common with his fellow Christians, that war was no longer permitted to him, he threw down his belt at the head of the legion, declaring

† Pol. Ep. and Phil. C. 2.—Evidences of Christianity.

that he had become a Christian, and that he would serve no longer. He was committed to prison; but he was still faithful to Christianity. "It is not lawful," said he, "for a Christian to bear arms for any earthly consideration;" and he was in consequence put to death. Almost immediately afterwards, Cassian, who was notary to the same legion, gave up his office. He steadfastly maintained the sentiments of Marcellus, and like him was consigned to the executioner. Martin, of whom so much is said by Sulpicius Severus, was bred to the profession of arms, which, on his acceptance of Christianity, he abandoned. To Julian the apostate, the only reason that we find he gave for his conduct was this,—"I am a Christian, and therefore I cannot fight." The answer of Tarachus to Numerianus Maximus is in words nearly similar:—"I have led a military life, and am a Roman; and because I am a Christian, I have abandoned my profession of a soldier."

These were not the sentiments, and this was not the conduct, of the insulated individuals who might be actuated by individual opinions, or by their private interpretations of the duties of Christianity. Their principles were the principles of the body. They were recognized and defended by the Christian writers their contemporaries. Justin Martyr and Tatian talk of soldiers and Christians as distinct characters; and Tatian says that the Christians declined even military commands. Clemens of Alexandria calls his Christian contemporaries the "Followers of Peace," and expressly tells us that "the followers of peace used none of the implements of war." Lactantius, another early Christian, says expressly, "It can *never* be lawful for a righteous man to go to war." About the end of the second century, Celsus, one of the opponents of Christianity, charged the Christians *with refusing to bear arms even in case of necessity.* Origen, the defender of the Christians, does not think of denying the fact; he admits the refusal, and justifies it, *because war was unlawful.* Even after Christianity had spread over almost the whole of the known world, Tertullian, in speaking of a part of the Roman armies, including more than one third of the standing legions of Rome, distinctly informs us that "not a Christian could be found amongst them."

All this is explicit. The evidence of the following facts is, however, yet more determinate and satisfactory. Some of the arguments which, at the present day, are brought against the advocates of peace, were then urged against these early Christians; and *these arguments they examined and repelled.* This indicates investigation and inquiry, and manifests that their belief of the unlawfulness of war was not a vague opinion, hastily admitted, and loosely floating amongst them; but that it was the result of deliberate examination, and a consequent firm conviction that Christ had forbidden it. Tertullian says, "Though the soldiers came to John, and received a certain form to be observed, yet Jesus Christ, by disarming Peter, disarmed every soldier afterwards; for custom never sanctions any unlawful act." "Can a soldier's life be lawful," says he in another work, "when Christ has pronounced that he who lives by the sword shall perish by the sword? Can any one who possesses the peacable doctrine of the gospel be a soldier, when it is his duty not so much as to go to law? And shall he, who is not to revenge his own wrongs, be instrumental in bringing others into chains, imprisonment, torture, death?" So that the very same arguments which are brought in defence of war at the present day, were brought against the Christians sixteen hundred years ago; and sixteen hundred years ago, they were repelled by these faithful contenders for the purity of our religion. It is remarkable, too, that Tertullian appeals to the precepts from the mount, in proof of those principles on which this Essay has been insisting:—*that the dispositions which the precepts inculcate are not compatible with war, and that war, therefore, is irreconcileable with Christianity.*

If it be possible, a still stronger evidence of the primitive belief is contained in the circumstance, that some of the Christian authors *declared that the refusal of the Christians to bear arms,* was a fulfilment of ancient prophecy. The peculiar strength of this evidence consists in this—that the fact of a refusal to bear arms is assumed as notorious and unquestioned. Irenæus, who lived about anno 180, affirms that the prophecy of Isaiah, which declared that men should turn their swords into ploughshares, and their spears into pruning hooks, *had been fulfilled in his time:* "for the Christians," says he, "have changed their swords and their lances into instruments of peace, and they *know not now how to fight.*" Justin Martyr, his contemporary, writes,—" That the prophecy is fulfilled, you have good reason to believe, for we, who in times past killed one another, *do not now fight with our enemies.*"

Tertullian, who lived later, says, " You must confess that the prophecy has been accomplished, as far as *the practice of every individual is concerned*, to whom it is applicable."*

It has been sometimes said, that the motive which influenced the early Christians to refuse to engage in war, consisted in the idolatry which was connected with the Roman armies. One motive this idolatry unquestionably afforded; but it is obvious, from the quotations which we have given, that their belief of the unlawfulness of *fighting*, independent of any question of idolatry, was an insuperable objection to engaging in war. Their words are explicit: "I cannot *fight* if I die."—"I am a Christian, and, therefore, I cannot *fight.*"—" Christ," says Tertullian, "*by disarming Peter*, disarmed every soldier;" and Peter was not about to fight in the armies of idolatry. So entire was their conviction of the incompatibility of war with our religion, that they would not even *be present* at the gladiatorial fights, " lest," says Theophilus, " we should become partakers of the murders committed there." Can any one believe that they who would not even *witness* a battle between two men, would themselves fight in a battle between armies? And the destruction of a gladiator, it should be remembered, was authorized by the state as much as the destruction of enemies in war.

It is, therefore, indisputable, that the Christians who lived nearest to the time of our Saviour, believed, with undoubting confidence, that he had unequivocally forbidden war—that they openly avowed this belief, and that, in support of it, they were willing to sacrifice, and did sacrifice, their fortunes and their lives.

* These examples might be multiplied. Enough, however, have been given to establish our position; and the reader who desires further or more immediate information, is referred to *Justin Mart.* in Dialog. cum Tryph. ejusdemque Apolog. 2. —ad Zenam : *Tertull.* de corona militis.—Apolog. cap. 21 and 37.—lib. de Idolol. c. 17, 18, 19.—ad Scapulam cap. 1.—adversus Jud. cap. 7 and 9.—adv. Gnost. 13. —adv. Marc. c. 4.—lib. de patient, c. 6. 10 : *Orig.* cont. *Celsum* lib. 3, 5, 8.—In Josuam hom. 12. cap. 9.—In Mat. cap. 26. tract. 36 : *Cypr.* Epist. 56—ad Cornel. Lactan. de just. lib 5. c. 18. lib. 6. c. 20 : *Ambr.* in Luc. 22. *Chrysost.* in Matth. 5, hom. 18.—in Matth. 26. hom. 85.—lib. 2 de Sacerdotio.—1 Cor. 13 : *Cromat.* in Matth. 5. *Hieron.* ad Ocean.—lib. Epist. p. 3. tom. 1. Ep. 2 ; *Athan.* de Inc. Verb. Dei : *Cyrill. Alex.* lib. 11. in Johan. cap. 25, 26. See also *Erasmus.* Luc. cap. 3, and 22. Ludov. Vives in Introd. ad Sap : *I Ferus* lib. 4. Comment in Mattu. 7 and Luc. 22.

Christians, however, afterwards became soldiers.—And when? When their *general* fidelity to Christianity became relaxed;—when, *in other respects,* they violated its principles;—when they had begun "to dissemble," and "to falsify their word," and "to cheat;"—when "Christian casuists" had persuaded them that they might "*sit at meat in the idol's temple;*"—when Christians accepted even *the priesthoods of idolatry.* In a word, they became soldiers, when they had ceased to be Christians.

The departure from the original faithfulness was, however, not suddenly general. Like every other corruption, war obtained by degrees. During the first two hundred years, not a Christian soldier is upon record. In the third century, when Christianity became partially corrupted, Christian soldiers were common. The number increased with the increase of the general profligacy; until at last, in the fourth century, Christians became soldiers without hesitation, and, perhaps, without remorse. Here and there, however, an ancient father still lifted up his voice for peace; but these, one after another, dropping from the world, the tenet that *war is unlawful,* ceased at length to be a tenet of the church.

Such was the origin of the present belief in the lawfulness of war. It began in unfaithfulness, was nurtured by profligacy, and was confirmed by general corruption. We seriously then, and solemnly invite the conscientious Christian of the present day, to consider these things. Had the professors of Christianity continued in the purity and faithfulness of their forefathers, we should *now* have believed that war was forbidden, and Europe, many long centuries ago, would have reposed in peace.

Let it always be borne in mind by those who are advocating war, that they are contending for a corruption which their forefathers abhorred; and that they are making Jesus Christ the sanctioner of crimes which his purest followers offered up their lives because they would not commit.

An argument has sometimes been advanced in favor of war from the Divine communications to the Jews under the administration of Moses. It has been said that as wars were allowed and enjoined to that people, they cannot be inconsistent with the will of God.

We have no intention to dispute, that, under the Mosaic dispensation, some wars were allowed, or that they were enjoined upon the Jews as an imperative duty. But those who refer, in justification of our present practice, to the authority by which the Jews prosecuted their wars, must be expected to produce the same authority for our own. Wars were *commanded* to the Jews, but are they commanded to us? War, in the abstract, was never commanded. And surely, those specific wars which were enjoined upon the Jews for an express purpose, are neither authority nor example for us, who have received no such injunction, and can plead no such purpose.

It will, perhaps, be said that the commands to prosecute wars, even to extermination, are so positive and so often repeated, that it is not probable, if they were inconsistent with the will of Heaven, they would have been thus peremptorily enjoined. We answer, that they were not inconsistent with the will of Heaven *then*. But even then, the prophets foresaw that they were not accordant with the universal will of God, since they predicted that when that will should be fulfilled, war should be eradicated from the world. And by what dispensation was this will to be fulfilled? By that of the "Rod out of the stem of Jesse."

But what do those who refer to the dispensation of Moses maintain? Do they say that the injunctions to the Jews are binding upon them? If they say this, we have at least reason to ask them for greater consistency of obedience. That these injunctions, in point of fact, do not bind them, they give sufficient proof, by the neglect of the greater portion of them, enforced as those injunctions were, by the same authority as that which commanded war. They have, therefore, so far as their argument is concerned, annulled the injunctions by their own rejection of them. And out of ten precepts to reject nine and retain one, is a gratuitous and idle mode of argument.

If I be told that we still acknowledge the obligation of many of these precepts, I answer that we acknowledge the duties which they enjoin, but not because of the authority which enjoined them. We obey the injunctions, not because they were delivered under the law, but because they are enforced by Christianity The command, "Thou shalt not kill," has never been abolished; but Christians do not prohibit murder because it was denounced in the decalogue, they would have prohibited it if the decalogue had never existed.

But farther: Some of the commands under the law, Christianity *requires* us to disobey. "*If a man have a stubborn and rebellious son, which will not obey the voice of his father, &c. all the men of the city shall stone him with stones that he die.** *If thy brother, the son of thy mother, or thy son, or thy daughter, or the wife of thy bosom, entice thee secretly, saying, 'Let us go and serve other gods,' thou shalt not pity him or conceal him, but thou shalt surely kill him; thine hand shall be first upon him to put him to death.*"† Now we know that Christianity will not sanction an obedience of these commands; and if we did obey them, our own laws would treat us as murderers. If the precepts under the dispensation of Moses are binding because they were promulgated by Heaven, they are binding in all their commands and all their prohibitions. But some of these precepts we habitually disregard, and some it were criminal to obey; and with what reason then do we refer to them in our defence?

And *why* was the law superseded? Because it "made nothing perfect."—"The law was given by Moses, but grace and *truth* came by Jesus Christ." The manner in which the author of "truth" prefaced some of his most important precepts is much to our present purpose. "It hath been said by them of old time, an eye for an eye," &c. He then introduces his own precept with the contradistinguishing preface—"But *I* say unto you." This, therefore, appears to be a specific abrogation of the *authority* of the legal injunctions, and an introduction of another system; and this is all that our present purpose requires. The truth is, that the law was abolished because of its imperfections; yet we take hold of one of these imperfections in justification of our present practice. Is it because we feel that we cannot defend it by our own religion?

We therefore dismiss the dispensation of Moses from any participation in the argument. Whatever it allowed, or whatever it prohibited in relation to war, we do not inquire. We ask only what Christianity allows and prohibits, and by this we determine the question.—It is the more necessary to point out the inapplicability of these arguments from the Old Testament, because there are some persons of desultory modes of thinking, who find that

---

* Deut. xxi. 18, 21.   † Deut. xiii. 9.

war is allowed in "the Bible," and who forget to inquire into the present authority of the permission.

There are some persons who suppose themselves sufficiently justified in their approbation of war, by the example of men of piety of our own times. The argument, as an argument, is of little concern; but every thing is important that makes us acquiescent in war. *Here are men,* say they, *who make the knowledge of their duties the great object of their study, and yet these men engage in war without any doubt of its lawfulness.* All this is true; and it is true also, that some good men have expressly inculcated the lawfulness of war; and it is true also, that the articles of the Church of England specifically assert it. But what, if it should have come to pass that "blindness in part, hath happened unto Israel?"

What is the argument? *That good men have engaged in war, and therefore that Christianity allows it.* They who satisfy themselves with such reasoning, should bear in mind that he who voluntarily passes over the practice of the first two centuries of Christianity, and attempts to defend himself by the practice of after and darker ages, has obviously no other motive than that he finds his religion, when vitiated and corrupt, more suitable to his purpose than it was in the days of its purity. This state of imperfection and impurity has diffused an influence upon the good, as upon the bad. I question not that some Christians of the present day who defend war, *believe* they act in accordance with their religion : just as I question not that many, who zealously bore faggots to the stake of the Christian martyrs, *believed* so too. The time has been, when those who killed good men *thought* "they did God service." But let the succeeding declaration be applied by our present objectors,—" These things will they do unto you, *because they have not known the Father nor Me.*"* Here, then, appears to be our error—that we do not estimate the conduct of men by the standard of the gospel, but that we reduce the standard of the gospel to the conduct of men. That good men should fail to conform to the perfect purity of Christianity, or to *perceive* it, need not be wondered, for we have sufficient examples of it. Good men in past ages allowed many things as permitted by Christian-

---

* John xvi. 3.

ity, which we condemn, and shall for ever condemn. In the present day there are many questions of duty on which men of piety disagree. If their authority be rejected by us on other points of practice, why is it to determine the question of war? Especially why do we insist on their decisions, when they differ in their decisions themselves? If good men have allowed the lawfulness of war, good men have also denied it. We are therefore again referred to the simple evidence of religion: an evidence which it will always be found wise to admit, and dangerous to question.

There is, however, one argument brought against us, which, if it be just, precludes at once all question upon the subject:—*That a distinction is to be made between rules which apply to us as individuals, and rules which apply to us as subjects of the state; and that the pacific injunctions of Christ from the mount, and all the other kindred commands and prohibitions of the Christian Scriptures, have no reference to our conduct as members of the political body.* This is the argument to which the greatest importance is attached by the advocates of war, and by which thinking men are chiefly induced to acquiesce in its lawfulness. In reality, some of those who think most acutely upon the subject, acknowledge that the peaceable, forbearing, forgiving dispositions of Christianity, are absolutely obligatory upon individuals in their full extent; and this acknowledgment I would entreat the reader to bear in his recollection.

Now it is obvious that the proof of the rectitude of this distinction, must be expected of those who make it. General rules are laid down by Christianity, of which, in some cases, the advocate of war denies the applicability. He, therefore, is to produce the reason and the authority for exception. Now we would remind him that general rules are binding, unless their inapplicability can be clearly shown. We would remind him that the general rules in question, are laid down by the commissioned ministers of Jesus Christ, and by Jesus Christ himself; and we would recommend him, therefore, to hesitate before he institutes exceptions to those rules, upon any authority *inferior* to the authority which made them.

The foundation for the distinction between the duties of Individuals and those of Communities, must, we suppose, be sought in one of these two positions:

1. That as no law exists, of general authority amongst nations, by which one state is protected from the violence of another, it is necessary that each independent community should protect itself; and that the security of a nation cannot sometimes be maintained otherwise than by war.

2. That as the general utility and expediency of actions is the foundation of their moral qualities, and as it is sometimes most conducive to general utility and expediency that there should be a war, war is, therefore, sometimes lawful.

The first of these positions will probably be thus enforced. If an individual suffers aggression, there is a Power to which he can apply that is above himself and above the aggressor; a power by which the bad passions of those around him are restrained, or by which their aggressions are punished. But amongst nations there is no acknowledged superior or common arbitrator.—Even if there were, there is no way in which its decisions could be enforced, but by the sword. War, therefore, is the only means which one nation possesses of protecting itself from the aggression of another.

This, certainly, is plausible reasoning; but it happens to this argument as to many others, that it assumes *that* as established, which has not been proved, and upon the proof of which the truth of the whole argument depends. It assumes, That the reason why an individual is not permitted to use violence, is, *that the laws will use it for him.* And in this the fallacy of the position consists; for the foundation of the duty of forbearance in private life, is *not* that the laws will punish aggression, but *that Christianity requires forbearance.* Undoubtedly, if the existence of a common arbitrator were the foundation of the duty, the duty would not be binding upon nations. But that which we require to be proved is this—that Christianity exonerates nations from those duties which she has imposed upon individuals. This, the present argument does not prove; and, in truth, with a singular unhappiness in its application, it assumes, in effect, that she has imposed these duties upon neither the one nor the other.

If it be said that Christianity allows to individuals some degree and kind of resistance, and that some resistance is therefore lawful to states, we do not deny it. But if it be said that the degree of lawful resistance extends to the slaughter of our fellow Christions what it extends to war, we do deny it: We say that the rules of Christianity cannot, by any possible latitude of interpretation, be made to extend to it. The duty of forbearance then, is *antecedent* to all considerations respecting the condition of man; and whether he be under the protection of laws or not, the duty of forbearance is imposed.

The only truth which appears to be elicited by the present argument, is, that the difficulty of obeying the forbearing rules of Christianity, is *greater* in the case of nations than in the case of individuals: *The obligation to obey them is the same in both.* Nor let any one urge the difficulty of obedience in opposition to the duty; for he who does this has yet to learn one of the most awful rules of his religion—a rule that was enforced by the precepts, and more especially by the final example, of Christ, of apostles, and of martyrs, the rule which requires that we should be "obedient even unto death."

Let it not, however, be supposed that we believe the difficulty of forbearance would be as great in practice as it is great in theory. We hope hereafter to show that it promotes our interests as certainly as it fulfils our duties.

The rectitude of the distinction between rules which apply to individuals and rules which apply to states, is thus maintained by Dr. Paley on the principle of EXPEDIENCY.

"The *only* distinction," says he, "that exists between the case of independent states and independent individuals, is founded in this circumstance: that the particular consequence sometimes appears to exceed the value of the general rule;" or, in less technical words, that a greater disadvantage may arise from obeying the commands of Christianity, than from transgressing them. *Expediency*, it is said, is the test of moral rectitude, and the standard of our duty. If we believe that it will be most expedient to disregard the general obligations of Christianity, that belief is the justifying motive of disregarding them. Dr. Paley proceeds to say, "In the transactions of private persons, no advantage that results from the breach of a general law of justice, can compensate to the public for the violation of the law; *in the concerns of empire* this *may sometimes be doubted.*" He says there may be cases in which "the magnitude of the particular evil induces us to *call in question* the obligation of the general rule." "Situations *may be feigned,* and consequently *may possibly arise,* in which the general tendency is outweighed by the enormity of the particular mischief." Of the doubts which must arise as to the occasions when the "obligation" of Christian laws ceases, he however says that "moral philosophy furnishes no precise solution;" and he candidly acknowledges "the danger of leaving it to the sufferer to decide upon the comparison of particular and general consequences, and the still greater danger of such decisions being drawn into future precedents. If treaties, for instance, be no longer binding than while they are convenient, or until the inconveniency ascend to a certain point (which point must be fixed by the judgment, or rather by the feelings of the complaining party),—one, and almost the only method of averting or closing the calamities of war, of preventing or putting a stop to the destruction of mankind, is lost to the world for ever." And in retrospect of the indeterminateness of these rules of conduct, he says finally, "these, however, are the principles upon which the calculation is to be formed."*

It is obvious that this reasoning proceeds upon the principle that *it is lawful to do evil that good may come.* If good will come by violating a treaty, we may violate it.† If good will come by slaughtering other men, we may slaughter them. I know that the advocate of expediency will tell us that it is *not* evil of which good, in the aggregate, comes; and that the good or evil of actions *consists* in the good or evil of their general consequences.—I appeal to the understanding and the conscience of the reader—Is this distinction honest to the meaning of the apostle? Did he intend to tell his readers that they might violate their solemn promises, that they might destroy their fellow Christians, *in order that good might come?* If he did mean this, surely there was little truth in the declaration of the same apostle, *that he used great plainness of speech.*

We are told that "whatever is *expedient* is right." We shall not quarrel with the dogma, but how is expediency to be determined? By the calculations and guessings of men, or by the knowledge and foresight of God? Expediency may be the

---

* Moral and Political Philosophy, Chap. "Of War and Military Establishments." † Ibid.

test of our duties, but what is the test of expediency?—Obviously I think, it is this; *the decisions which God has made known respecting what is best for man.* Calculations of expediency, of "particular and general consequences," are not intrusted to us, for this most satisfactory reason—that we cannot make them. The calculation, to be any thing better than vague guessing, requires prescience, and where is prescience to be sought? Now it is conceded by our opponents, that the only possessor of prescience has declared that the forbearing, non-resisting character *is* best for man. Yet we are told, that sometimes it is *not* best, that sometimes it is "inexpedient." How do we discover this? The promulgator of the law has never intimated it. Whence, then, do we derive the right of substituting our computations for His prescience? Or, having obtained it, what is the limit to its exercise? If, because we calculate that obedience will not be beneficial, we may dispense with his laws in one instance, why may we not dispense with them in ten? Why may we not abrogate them altogether?

The right is however claimed; and how is it to be exercised? We are told that the duty of obedience "may sometimes be *doubted*"—that in some cases, we are induced to "*call in question*" the obligation of the Christian rule—that "situations *may be feigned*,"—that circumstances "*may possibly arise,*" in which we are at liberty to dispense with it—that still it is dangerous to leave "it to the sufferer to decide" when the obligation of the rule ceases; and that of all these doubts "philosophy furnishes no precise solution!"—I know not how to contend against such principles as these. An argument might be repelled; the assertion of a fact might be disproved; but what answer can be made to "possibilities" and "doubts?" They who are at liberty to *guess* that Christian laws may sometimes be suspended, are at liberty to guess that Jupiter is a fixed star, or that the existence of America is a fiction. What answer the man of science would make to such suppositions I do not know, and I do not know what answer to make to ours. Amongst a community which had to decide on the "particular and general consequences" of some political measure, which involved the sacrifice of the principles of Christianity, there would of necessity be an endless variety of opinions. Some would think it *expedient* to supersede the law of Christianity, and some would think the evil of obeying the law less than the evil of transgressing it. Some would think that the "particular mischief" outweighed the "general rule," and some that the "general rule" outweighed the "particular mischief." And in this chaos of opinion, what is the line of rectitude, or how is it to be discovered? Or, is *that* rectitude, which appears to each separate individual to be right? And are there as many species of truth as there are discordancies of opinion?—Is *this* the simplicity of the gospel? Is *this* the path in which a wayfaring man, though a fool, shall not err?

These are the principles of expediency on which it is argued that the duties which attach to private life do not attach to citizens.—I think it will be obvious to the eye of candour, that they are exceedingly indeterminate and vague. Little more appears to be done by Dr. Paley than to exhibit their doubtfulness. In truth, I do not know whether he has argued better in favour of his position, or against it. To me it appears that he has evinced it to be fallacious; for I do not think that *any thing* can be Christian truth, of which the truth cannot be more evidently proved. But whatever may be thought of the conclusion, the reader will certainly perceive that the whole question is involved in extreme vagueness and indecision: an indecision and vagueness, which it is difficult to conceive that Christianity ever intended should be hung over the very greatest question of practical morality that man has to determine; over the question that asks whether the followers of Christ are at liberty to destroy one another. That such a procedure as a war is, under any circumstances, sanctioned by Christianity, from whose principles it is acknowledged to be "abhorrent," ought to be clearly made out. It ought to be obvious to loose examination. It ought not to be necessary to ascertaining it, that a critical investigation should be made, of questions which ordinary men cannot comprehend, and which, if they comprehended them, they could not determine; and above all, that investigation ought not to end, as we have seen it does end, in vague indecision—in "doubts" of which even "Philosophy furnishes no precise solution." But when this indecision and vagueness are brought to oppose the Christian evidence for peace; when it is contended, not only that it militates against that evidence, but that it outbalances and supersedes it—we would say of such an argument, that it is not only weak, but idle; of such a conclusion, that it is not only unsound, but preposterous.

Christian obligation is a much more simple thing than speculative philosophy would make it appear; and to all those who suppose that our relations as subjects dismiss the obligation of Christian laws, we would offer the consideration, that neither the Founder of Christianity nor his apostles ever made the distinction. Of questions of "particular and general consequences," of "general advantages and particular mischiefs," no traces are to be found in their words or writings. The morality of Christianity is a simple system, adapted to the comprehensions of ordinary men. Were it otherwise, what would be its usefulness? If philosophers only could examine our duties, and if their examinations ended in *doubts without solution*, how would men, without learning and without leisure, regulate their conduct? I think, indeed, that it is a sufficient objection to all such theories as the present, that they are not adapted to the wayfaring man. If the present theory be admitted, one of these two effects will be the consequence: the greater part of the community must trust for the discovery of their duties to the sagacity of others, or they must act without any knowledge of their duties at all.

But, that the pacific injunctions of the Christian Scriptures do apply to us, under every circumstance of life, whether private or public, appears to be made necessary by the universality of Christian obligation. The language of Christianity upon the obligation of her moral laws, is essentially this,—" What I say unto you, I say unto all." The pacific laws of our religion, then, are binding upon all men; upon the king and upon every individual who advises him, upon every member of a legislature, upon every officer and agent, and upon every private citizen. How then can *that* be lawful for a body of men which is unlawful for each individual? How if one be disobedient, can his offence make disobedience lawful to all? We maintain yet more, and say, that to dismiss Christian benevolence as subjects, and to retain it as individuals, is simply impossible. He who possesses that subjugation of the affections and that universality of benevolence, by which he is influenced to do good to those who hate him, and to love his enemies in private life, cannot, without abandoning those dispositions, butcher other men because they are called public enemies.

The whole position, therefore, that the pacific commands and prohibitions of the Christian Scriptures do not apply to our conduct as subjects of a state, appears to me to be a fallacy. Some of the arguments which are brought to support it, so flippantly dispense with the principles of Christian obligation, so gratuitously assume, that because obedience may be difficult, obedience is not required, that they are rather an excuse for the distinction than a justification of it—and some are so lamentably vague and indeterminate, the principles which are proposed are so technical, so inapplicable to the circumstance of society, and in truth, so incapable of being practically applied, that it is not credible that they were designed to suspend the obligation of rules which were imposed by a revelation from Heaven.

The reputation of Dr. Paley is so great, that, as he has devoted a chapter of the Moral Philosophy to "War and Military Establishments," it will perhaps be expected, in an inquiry like the present, that some specific reference should be made to his opinions; and I make this reference willingly.

The chapter "on War" begins thus:—"Because the Christian Scriptures describe wars, as what they are, as crimes or judgments, some men have been led to believe that it is unlawful for a Christian to bear arms. But it should be remembered, that it may be necessary for individuals to unite their force, and for this end to resign themselves to a common will; and yet it may be true that that will is often actuated by criminal motives, and often determined to destructive purposes." This is a most remarkable paragraph: It assumes, at once, the whole subject of inquiry, and is an assumption couched in extraordinary laxity of language.—"It may be necessary for individuals to unite their force." The tea-table and the drawing-room have often told us this: but *philosophy* should tell us how the necessity is proved. Nor is the morality of the paragraph more rigid than the philosophy,—"Wars are crimes," and are often undertaken from "criminal motives, and determined to destructive purposes;" yet of these purposes, and motives, and crimes, "it may be necessary' for Christians to become the abettors and accomplices!

Paley proceeds to say, that in the New Testament *the profession of a soldier** is nowhere forbidden or condemned; and he refers to the case of John the Baptist, of the Roman centurion, and of Cornelius; and with this he finishes all inquiry into the Christian evidence upon the subject, after having expended upon it less than a page of the edition before me.

These arguments are all derived from the silence of the New Testament, and to all reasoning founded upon this silence, no one can give a better answer than himself. In replying to the defences by which the advocates of slavery attempt to justify it, he notices that which they advance from *the silence of the New Testament* respecting it. He says—It is urged that "Slavery was a part of the civil constitution of most countries when Christianity appeared; yet that no passage is to be found in the Christian Scriptures, by which it is condemned or prohibited." "This," he rejoins, "is true; for Christianity, soliciting admission into all nations of the world, abstained, as behooved it, from intermeddling with the civil institutions of any. But does it follow, from the silence of Scriptures concerning them, that all the civil institutions which then prevailed were right; or that the bad should not be exchanged for better?" I beg the reader to apply this reasoning to Paley's own arguments in favour of war from the silence of the Scriptures. How happens it that he did not remember it himself?

Now I am compelled to observe, that in the discussion of the lawfulness of war, Dr. Paley has neglected his professed principles of decision and his ordinary practice. His professed principles are these; that the discovery of the "will of God, which is the whole business of morality," is to be attained by referring, *primarily*, to "his express declarations when they are to be had, and which must be sought for in Scripture."—Has he sought for these declarations? Has he sought for "Resist not evil," or for "Love your enemies," or for "Put up thy sword," or for "The

---

* I do not know why "the profession of a soldier" is substituted for the simple term, *war*. Dr. P. does not say that *war* is nowhere forbidden or condemned, which censure or prohibition it is obviously easy to have pronounced without even noticing "the profession of a soldier." I do not say that this language implies a want of ingenuousness, but it certainly was more easy to prove that the *profession of a soldier* is nowhere condemned, than that *war* is nowhere condemned.

weapons of our warfare are not carnal," or for " My kingdom is not of this world?" He has sought for none of these; he has examined none of them. He has noticed none of them. His professed principles are, again, that *when our instructions are dubious, we should endeavor to explain them by what we can collect of our Master's general inclination or intention.** Has he conformed to his own rule? Has he endeavored to collect this general inclination, and to examine this general tendency? He has taken no notice of it whatever. This neglect, we say, is contrary to his ordinary practice. Upon other subjects, he has assiduously applied to the Christian Scriptures in determination of truth. He has examined not only their direct evidence, but the evidence which they afford by induction and implication,—the evidence arising from their general tendency. Suicide is nowhere condemned in the New Testament; yet Paley condemns it, and how? He examines the sacred volume, and finds that by implication and inference, it may be collected that suicide is not permitted by Christianity. He says that patience under suffering is inculcated as an important duty; and that the recommendation of patience, implies the unlawfulness of suicide to get out of suffering. This is sound reasoning; but he does not adopt it in the examination of war. Could he not have found that the inculcation of peaceableness forms as good an argument against the lawfulness of war, as the inculcation of patience forms against the lawfulness of suicide? He certainly could have done this, and why has he not done it? Why has he passed it over in silence?

I must confess my belief, that he was unwilling to discuss the subject upon Christian principles; that he had resolved to make war consistent with Christianity; and that, foreseeing her "express declarations" and "general intentions" militated against it, he avoided noticing them at all. Thus much at least is certain, that in discussing the lawfulness of war, he has abandoned both his avowed principles and his correspondent practice. There is, to me at least, in the chapter "On War," an appearance of great indecision of mind, arising from the conflict between Christian truth and the power of habit,—between the consciousness that war is "abhorrent" to our religion, and the desire to defend it on the

---

* Moral and Political Philosophy, Book ii. Chap. 4.

principle of expediency. The whole chapter is characterized by a very extraordinary laxity both of arguments and principles.

After the defensibility of war has been proved, or assumed, in the manner which we have exhibited, Dr. Paley states the occasions upon which he determines that wars become justifiable. "The objects of *just* wars," says he, "are precaution, defence, or reparation."—" Every *just* war supposes an injury perpetrated, attempted, or feared."

I shall acknowledge, that if these be justifying motives to war, I see very little purpose in talking of morality upon the subject. It was wise to leave the principles of Christianity out of the question, and to pass them by unnoticed, if they were to be succeeded by principles like these. It is in vain to expatiate on moral obligations, if we are at liberty to declare war whenever an "injury is feared." An injury, without limit to its insignificance! A fear, without stipulation for its reasonableness! The judges, also, of the reasonableness of fear, are to be they who are under its influence; and who so likely to judge amiss as those who are afraid? Sounder philosophy than this has told us, that "he who has to reason upon his duty when the temptation to transgress it is before him, is almost sure to reason himself into an error." The necessity for this ill-timed reasoning, and the allowance of it, is amongst the capital objections to the philosophy of Paley. It tells us that a people may suspend the laws of God when they think it is "expedient;" and they are to judge of this expediency when the temptation to transgression is before them! —Has Christianity left the lawfulness of human destruction to be determined on such principles as these?

Violence, rapine, and ambition, are not to be restrained by morality like this. It may serve for the speculation of a study; but we will venture to affirm that mankind will never be controlled by it. Moral rules are useless, if, from their own nature, they cannot be, or will not be applied. Who believes that if kings and conquerors may fight when they have fears, they will not fight when they have them not? The morality allows too much latitude to the passions, to retain any practical restraint upon them. And a morality that will not be practised, I had almost said, that cannot be practised, is an useless morality. It is a *theory* of morals. We want clearer and more exclusive rules we want more obvious and immediate sanctions. It were in vain for a philosopher to say to a general who was burning for glory, "You are at liberty to engage in the war provided you have suffered, or fear you will suffer an injury: otherwise Christianity prohibits it." He will tell him of twenty injuries that have been suffered, of a hundred that have been attempted, and of ten thousand that he fears. And what answer can the philosopher make to him?

I think that Dr. Paley has, in another and a later work, given us stronger arguments in favour of peace than the Moral Philosophy gives in favour of war. In the "Evidences of Christianity" we find these statements:—"The two following positions appear to me to be satisfactorily made out: first, That the gospel *omits some qualities*, which have usually engaged the praises and admiration of mankind, but which, in reality, and in their general effects, have been *prejudicial to human happiness;* secondly, that the gospel has *brought forward some virtues*, which *possess the highest intrinsic value*, but which have commonly been overlooked and condemned.—The second of these propositions is exemplified in the instances of passive courage or endurance of suffering, patience under affronts and injuries, humility, irresistance, placability.—The truth is, there are two opposite descriptions of character under which mankind may be generally classed. The one possesses vigour, firmness, resolution, is daring and active, quick in its sensibilities, jealous in its fame, eager in its attachments, inflexible in its purpose, violent in its resentments. The other meek, yielding, complying, forgiving, not prompt to act, but willing to suffer, silent and gentle under rudeness and insult, suing for reconciliation where others would demand satisfaction, giving way to the pushes of impudence, conceding and indulgent to the prejudices, the wrong-headedness, the intractibility of those with whom it has to deal.—The former of these characters is, and ever hath been, the favourite of the world.—Yet so it hath happened, that with the Founder of Christianity, *this latter is the subject of his commendation, his precepts, his example;* and that *the former is so, in no part of its composition.* This morality shows, at least, that *no two things can be more different than the heroic and the Christian characters.* Now it is proved, in contradiction to first impressions, to popular opinion, to the encomiums of orators and poets, and even to the suffrages of historians and moralists, that *the latter character possesses most of true worth,* both as being most difficult either to be acquired or sustained, and as *contributing most to the happiness and tranquillity of social life.*—If this disposition were universal, the case is clear; the world would be a society of friends: whereas, if the other disposition were universal, it would produce a scene of universal contention. The world would not be able to hold a generation of such men. If, what is the fact, the disposition be partial; if a few be actuated by it amongst a multitude who are not, *in whatever degree it does prevail, it prevents, allays, and terminates quarrels, the great disturbers of human happiness, and the great sources of human misery,* so far as man's happiness and misery depend upon man. *The preference of the patient to the heroic character,* which we have here noticed, is a peculiarity in the Christian institution, which I propose as *an argument of wisdom."* *

These are the sentiments of Dr. Paley upon this great characteristic of the Christian morality. I think that in their plain, literal, and unsophisticated meaning, they exclude the possibility of the lawfulness of war. The simple conclusion from them is, that violence, and devastation, and human destruction cannot exist in conjunction with the character of a Christian. This would be the conclusion of the inhabitant of some far and peaceful island, where war and Christianity were alike unknown. If he read these definitions of the Christian duties, and were afterwards told that we thought ourselves allowed to plunder and to murder one another, he would start in amazement at the monstrous inconsistency. Casuistry may make her "distinctions," and philosophy

---

* I must be just. After these declarations, the author says, that when the laws which inculcate the Christian character, are applied to what is necessary to be done for the sake of the public, they are applied to a case to which they do not belong; and he adds, "This distinction is plain," but in what its plainness consists, or how it is discovered at all, he does not inform us. The reader will probably wonder, as I do, that whilst Paley says no two things can be more opposite than the Christian and the heroic characters, he nevertheless thinks it "is plain" that Christianity sanctions the latter.

I would take the opportunity afforded me by this note, to entreat the reader to look over the whole of Chap. 2, Part II., in the Evidences of Christianity. He will find many observations on the placability of the gospel, which will repay the time of reading them.

may talk of her "expediencies," but the monstrous inconsistency remains. What is the fact? Mahometans and Pagans do not believe that our religion allows of war. They reproach us with the inconsistency. Our wars are, with them, a scandal and a taunt. "You preach to us," say they, "of Christianity, and would convert us to your creed;—first convert yourselves; show us that yourselves believe in it." Nay, the Jews at our own doors tell us, that our wars are an evidence that the Prince of Peace is not come. They bring the violence of Christians to prove that Christ was a deceiver. Thus do we cause the way of truth to be evil spoken of. Thus, are we, who should be the helpers of the world, its stumbling-blocks and its shame. We, who should be lights to them that sit in darkness, cause them to love that darkness still. Well may the Christian be ashamed for these things: Well may he be ashamed for the reputation of his religion: And he may be ashamed too, for the honoured defender of the Christian faith who stands up, the advocate of blood; who subtilizes the sophisms of the schools, and roves over the fields of speculation to find an argument to convince us that we may murder one another! This is the "wisdom of the world;" that wisdom which is, emphatically, "FOOLISHNESS."

We have seen that the principle on which Dr. Paley's Moral Philosophy decides that war is lawful, is, that it is expedient. I know not how this argument accords with some of the statements of the Evidences of Christianity. We are there told that the non-resisting character " possesses the highest intrinsic value," and the "most of true worth;" that it "prevents the great disturbances of human happiness," and destroys "the great sources of human misery," and that it " contributes most to the happiness and tranquillity of social life." And in what then does expediency consist, if the non-resisting character be not expedient? Dr. Paley says, again, in relation to the immense mischief and bloodshed arising from the violation of Christian duty—" We do not say that no evil can exceed this, nor any possible advantage compensate it, but we say that a loss which affects all, *will scarcely be made up to the common stock of human happiness, by any benefit that can be procured to a single nation.*" And is not therefore the violation of the duty *inexpedient* as well as criminal? He says again that the warlike character " *is, in its* general effects, prejudicial to human happiness,—and therefore, surely, it is inexpedient.

The advocate of war, in the abundance of his topics of defence (or in the penury of them) has had recourse to this:— *That, as a greater number of male children are brought into the world than of female, wars are the ordination of Providence to rectify the inequality;* and one or two moralists have proceeded a step farther, and have told us, not that war is designed to carry off the excess, but *that an excess is born in order to supply its slaughters.* Dreadful! Are we to be told that God sends too many of his rational creatures into the world, and therefore that he stands in need of wars to destroy them? Has he no other means of adjusting the proportions of the species, than by a system which violates the revelation that he has made, and the duties that he has imposed? Or, yet more dreadful—are we to be told that He creates an excess of one of the sexes, on purpose that their destruction of each other may be with impunity to the species. This reasoning surely is sufficiently confident:—I fear it is more than sufficiently profane. But alas for the argument! It happens most unfortunately for it, that although more males are born than females, yet from the greater mortality of the former, it is found that long before the race arrives at maturity, the number of females predominates. What a pity—that just as the young men had grown old enough to kill one another, it should be discovered that there are not too many to remain peaceably alive! Let then, the principle be retained and acted upon; and since we have now an excess of females, let us send forth an armament of ladies that their redundance may be lopped by the appointed means.—But really it is time for the defender of war to abandon reasoning like this. It argues little in favor of any cause, that its advocates have recourse to such deplorable subterfuges.

The magistrate "beareth not the sword in vain; for he is the minister of God, a revenger to execute wrath upon him that doeth evil." From this acknowledgment of the lawfulness of coercion on the part of the civil magistrate, an argument has been advanced in favor of war. It is said, that by parity of reasoning, coercion is also lawful in the suppression of the violence which one nation uses towards another.

Some men talk as if the principles which we maintain were subversive of all order and government. They ask us—Is the civil magistrate to stand still and see lawless violence ravaging the land? Is the whole fabric of human society to be dissolved?

We answer, No; and that whencesoever these men may have derived their terrors, they are not chargeable upon us or upon our principles. To deduce even a plausible argument in favor of war from the permission, "to execute wrath upon him that doeth evil," it is obviously necessary to show that we are permitted to take his life. And the right to put an offender to death, must be proved, if it can be proved at all, either *from an express permission of the Christian Scriptures*, or, supposing Christianity to have given no decisions, either directly or indirectly, *from a necessity which knows no alternative*. Now every one knows that this express permission to inflict death is not to be found; and, upon the question of its *necessity*, we ask for that evidence which alone can determine it—the evidence of experience: and this evidence the advocate of war has never brought, and cannot bring. And we shall probably not be contradicted when we say that that degree of evidence which experience has afforded, is an evidence in our favor rather than against us.

But some persons entertain an opinion, that in the case of murder, at least, there is a sort of immutable necessity for taking the offender's life. "Whoso sheddeth man's blood, by man shall his blood be shed." If any one urges this rule against us, we reply, that it is not a rule of Christianity; and if the necessity of demanding blood for blood is an everlasting principle of retributive justice, how happens it that in the first case in which murder was committed, the murderer was not put to death?

The philosopher however would prove what the Christian cannot; and Mably accordingly says, "In the state of nature I have a right to take the life of him who lifts his arm against mine. *This right, upon entering into society, I surrender to the magistrate.*" If we conceded the truth of the first position, (which we do not,) the conclusion from it is a sophism too idle for notice. Having, however, been thus told that the state has a right to kill, we are next informed by Filangieri, that the criminal has no right to live. He says, "If I have a right to kill another man, *he has lost his* *right tc life."** Rousseau goes a little farther. He tells us that in consequence of the "social contract" which we make with the sovereign on entering into society, "Life is a conditional grant of the state ;"† so that we hold our lives, it seems, only as "tenants at will," and must give them up whenever their owner, the state, requires them. The reader has probably hitherto thought that he retained his head by some other tenure.

The right of taking an offender's life being thus proved, Mably shows us how its exercise becomes expedient. "A murderer," says he, "in taking away his enemy's life, *believes he does him the greatest possible evil.* Death, then, in the murderer's estimation, is the greatest of evils. *By the fear of death, therefore*, the excesses of hatred and revenge must be restrained." If language wilder than this can be held, Rousseau, I think, holds it. He says, "The preservation of both sides (the criminal and the state) is incompatible ; one of the two must perish." How it happens that a nation "must perish" if a convict is not hanged, the reader, I suppose, will not know.

I have referred to these speculations for the purpose of showing, that the right of putting offenders to death is not easily made out. Philosophers would scarcely have had recourse to these metaphysical abstractions if they knew an easier method of establishing the right. Even philosophy, however, concedes us much :—"*Absolute necessity, alone*," says Pastoret, " can justify the punishment of death ;" and Rousseau himself acknowledges, that, "we have no right to put to death, *even for the sake of example*, any but those who cannot be permitted to live without danger." Beccaria limits the right to two specific cases ; in which, "if an individual, though deprived of his liberty, has still such credit and connexions as may endanger the security of the nation, or, by his existence, is likely to produce a dangerous revolution in the established form of government—he must undoubtedly die."‡ It is not, perhaps, necessary for us to point out why, in these suppositious cases, a prisoner may not be put to death ; since I believe that philosophy will find it difficult, on some of her own principles, to justify his destruction : For Dr. Paley decides, that when-

---

* Montagu on Punishment of Death.   † Contr. Soc. ii. 5 Montagu.
‡ Del Delitti e delia Penes, xvi. Montagu.

ever a man thinks there are great grievances in the existing government, and that, by heading a revolt, he can redress them, without occasioning greater evil by the rebellion than benefit by its success—*it is his duty to rebel.** The prisoner whom Beccaria supposes, may be presumed to have thought this; and with reason too, for the extent of his credit, his connexions, and his success, is the plea for putting him to death; and we must therefore leave it to those who indulge in such speculations, to consider, how it can be right for one man to take the lead in a revolution, whilst it is right for another to hang him for taking it.

What then does the lawfulness of coercion on the part of the magistrate prove upon the question of the lawfulness of war? If capital punishments *had never been inflicted*, what would it have proved? Obviously nothing. If capital punishments *cannot be shown to be defensible*, what does it prove? Obviously nothing: for an unauthorized destruction of human life on the gallows, cannot justify another unauthorized destruction of it on the field.

Perhaps some of those who may have been hitherto willing to give me a patient attention, will be disposed to withdraw it, when they hear the unlawfulness of defensive war unequivocally maintained. But it matters not. My business is with what appears to me to be truth: if truth surprises us, I cannot help it—still it is truth.

Upon the question of defensive war, I would beg the reader to bear in his recollection, that every feeling of his nature is enlisted against us; and I would beg him, knowing this, to attain as complete an abstraction from the influence of those feelings as shall be in his power. This he will do, if he is honest in the inquiry for truth. It is not necessary to conceal that the principles which we maintain may sometimes demand the sacrifice of our apparent interests. Such sacrifices Christianity has been wont to require: they are the tests of our fidelity; and of those whom I address, I believe there are some, who, if they can be assured that we speak the language of Christianity, will require no other inducements to obedience.

The lawfulness of defensive war is commonly simplified to *The Right of Self-defence.* This is one of the strongholds of the

---

* Moral and Political Philosophy.

defender of war, the almost final fastness to which he retires. *The instinct of self-preservation,* it is said, *is an instinct of nature; and since this instinct is implanted by God, whatever is necessary to self-preservation is accordant with his will.* This is specious, but like many other specious arguments, it is sound in its premises, but, as I think, fallacious in its conclusions. That the instinct of self-preservation is an instinct of nature, is clear—that, because it is an instinct of nature, we have a right to kill other men, is *not* clear.

The fallacy of the whole argument appears to consist in this,— that it assumes that an instinct of nature is a law of *paramount* authority. God has implanted in the human system various propensities or instincts, of which the purposes are wise. These propensities tend in their own nature to *abuse;* and when gratified or followed to excess, they become subversive of the purposes of the wisdom which implanted them, and destructive of the welfare of mankind. He has therefore instituted a *superior law,* sanctioned by his immediate authority: by this law, we are required to regulate these propensities. The question therefore is, not whether the instinct of self-preservation is implanted by nature but whether Christianity has restricted its operation. By this, and by this only, the question is to be determined. Now he who will be at the trouble of making the inquiry, will find that a regulation of the instincts of nature, and a restriction of their exercise, is a prominent object of the Christian morality; and I think it is plain that this regulation and restriction apply to the instinct before us. That some of these propensities are to be restrained is certain. One of the most powerful instincts of our nature, is an affection to which the regulating precepts of Christianity are peculiarly directed. I do not maintain that any natural instinct is to be eradicated, but that all of them are to be regulated and restrained; and I maintain this of the instinct of self-preservation.

The establishment of this position is, indeed, the great object of the present inquiry. What are the dispositions and actions to which the instinct of self-preservation prompts, but actions and dispositions which Christianity forbids? They are non-forbearance, resistance, retaliation of injuries. The truth is, that it is to *defence* that the peaceable precepts of Christianity are directed.

Offence appears not to have even suggested itself. It is "Resist not evil;" it is "Overcome *evil* with good;" it is "Do good to them that hate you;" it is "Love your *enemies*;" it is "Render not evil for *evil*;" it is "Whoso *smiteth thee on one cheek.*" All this supposes previous offence, or injury, or violence; and it is *then* that forbearance is enjoined.

"The chief aim," says a judicious author, "of those who argue in behalf of defensive war, is directed *at the passions;*"* and accordingly, the case of an assassin will doubtless be brought against me. I shall be asked—Suppose a ruffian breaks into your house, and rushes into your room with his arm lifted to murder you, do you not believe that Christianity allows you to kill him? This is the last refuge of the cause: my answer to it is explicit—*I do not believe it.*

I have referred to this utmost possible extremity, because I am willing to meet objections of whatever nature, and because, by stating this, which is enforced by all our prejudices and all our instincts, I shall at least show that I give to those who differ from me, a fair, an open, and a candid recognition of all the consequences of my principles. I would, however, beg the same candour of the reader, and remind him, that were they unable to abide this test, the case of the ruffian has little practical reference to war. I remind him of this, not because I doubt whether our principles can be supported, but because, if he should think that in this case I do not support them, he will yet recollect that very few wars are proved to be lawful.—Of the wars which are prosecuted, some are simply wars of aggression; some are for the maintenance of a balance of power; some are in assertion of technical rights, and some, undoubtedly to repel invasion. The last are perhaps the fewest; and of these only it can be said that they bear any analogy whatever to the case which is supposed; and even in these, the analogy is seldom complete. It has rarely indeed happened that wars have been undertaken simply for the preservation of life, and that no other alternative has remained to a people, than to kill or to be killed. And let it be remembered, that *unless this alternative only remains,* the case of the ruffian is irrelevant; it applies not, practically to the subject.

* "The Lawfulness of Defensive War impartially considered, by a Member of the Church of England."

I do not know what those persons mean, who say, that we are authorized to kill an assassin by *the law of nature.* Principles like this, heedlessly assumed, as of self-evident truth, are, I believe, often the starting-post of our errors, the point of divergency from rectitude, from which our after obliquities proceed. Some men seem to talk of the laws of nature, as if nature were a legislatress who had sat and framed laws for the government of mankind. Nature makes no laws. A law implies a legislator; and there is no legislator upon the principles of human duty, but God. If, by the "law of nature," is meant any thing of which the sanctions or obligations are *different* from those of revelation, it is obvious that we have set up a moral system of our own, and in opposition to that which has been established by Heaven. If we mean by the "law of nature," nothing but that which is *accordant* with revelation, to what purpose do we refer to it at all? I do not suppose that any sober moralist will statedly advance the laws of nature in opposition to the laws of God; but I think that to advance them *at all*—that to refer to *any* principle or law, in determination of our duty, irrespectively of the simple will of God, is always dangerous: for there will be many, who, when they are referred for direction to such law or principle, will regard it, in their practice, as a *final* standard of truth. I believe that a reference to the laws of nature has seldom illustrated our duties, and never induced us to perform them; and that it has hitherto answered little other purpose than that of amusing the lovers of philosophical morality.

The mode of proving, or of stating, the right to kill an assassin, is this:—" There is one case in which all extremities are justifiable; namely, when our life is assaulted, and it becomes necessary for our preservation to kill the assailant. This is evident in a state of nature; unless it can be shown that we are bound to prefer the aggressor's life to our own; that is to say, to love our enemy *better* than ourselves, which can never be a debt of justice, nor any where appears to be a duty of charity."* If I were disposed to hold argumentation like this, I would say, that although we may not be required to love our enemies *better* than ourselves, we are required to love them *as* ourselves; and that in the sup-

* Moral and Political Philosophy.

posed case, it still would be a question equally balanced, which life ought to be sacrificed; for it is quite clear, that if we kill the assailant, we love him *less* than ourselves, which may, perhaps, militate a little against "a duty of charity." But the truth is, that the question is not whether we should love our enemy better than ourselves, but whether we should sacrifice the laws of Christianity in order to preserve our lives—whether we should prefer the interests of religion to our own—whether we should be willing to "lose our life, for Christ's sake and the gospel's."

This system of *counter-crime* is of very loose tendency. The assailant violates his duties by attempting to kill me, and I, therefore, am to violate mine by actually killing him. Is his meditated crime, then, a justification of my perpetrated crime? In the case of a condemned Christian martyr who was about to be led to the stake, it is supposable, that by having contrived a mine, he may preserve his life by suddenly firing it and blowing his persecutors into the air. Would Christianity justify the act? Or what should we say of him if he committed it? We should say that whatever his *faith* might be, his *practice* was very unsound; that he might *believe* the gospel, but that he certainly did not fulfil its duties. Now I contend that for all the purposes of the argument, the cases of the martyr and the assaulted person are precisely similar. He who was about to be led to the stake, and he who was about to lose his life by the assassin, are both required to regulate their conduct by the same laws, and are both to be prepared to offer up their lives in testimony of their allegiance to Christianity: the one in allegiance to her, in opposition to the violation of her moral principles and her moral spirit; and the other, in opposition to errors in belief or to ecclesiastical corruptions. It is therefore in vain to tell me that the victim of persecution would have suffered for religion's sake, for so also would the victim of the ruffian. There is nothing in the sanctions of Christianity which implies that obedience to her moral law is of less consequence than an adherence to her faith; nor, as it respects the welfare of the world, does the consequence appear to be less; for he who, by his fidelity to Christianity, promotes the diffusion of Christian dispositions and of peace, contributes, perhaps, as much to the happiness of mankind, as he who by the same fidelity recommends the acceptance of an accurate creed.

A great deal hangs upon this question, and it is therefore necessary to pursue it farther. We say, then, first—that Christianity has not declared that we are ever at liberty to kill other men: secondly—that she virtually prohibits it, because her principles and the practice of our Saviour are not compatible with it, and, thirdly—that if Christianity allowed it, she would in effect and in practice allow *war*, without restriction to defence of life.

The first of these positions will probably not be disputed; and upon the second, that Christianity virtually prohibits the destruction of human life, it has been the principal object of this essay to insist. I would, therefore, only observe, that the conduct of the Founder of Christianity, when his *enemies approached him " with swords and staves,"* appears to apply strictly to self-defence. These armed men came with the final purpose of murdering him; but although he knew this purpose, he would not suffer the assailants to be killed or even to be wounded. Christ, therefore, would not preserve his own life by sacrificing another's.

But we say, thirdly, that if Christianity allows us to kill one another, in self-defence, she allows *war*, without restriction to self-defence. Let us try what would have been the result if the Christian Scriptures had thus placed human life at our disposal: suppose they had said—*You may kill a ruffian in your own defence, but you may not enter into a defensive war.* The prohibition would admit, not of *some* exceptions to its application—the exceptions would be so many, that no prohibition would be left; because there is no practical limit to the right of self-defence, until we arrive at defensive war. If one man may kill one, two may kill two, and ten may kill ten, and an army may kill an army:—and this is defensive *war*. Supposing, again, the Christian Scriptures had said, *an army may fight in its own defence, but not for any other purpose.* We do not say that the exceptions to *this* rule would be so many as wholly to nullify the rule itself; but we say that whoever will attempt to apply it in practice, will find that he has a very wide range of justifiable warfare; a range that will embrace many more wars than moralists, laxer than we shall suppose him to be, are willing to defend. If an army may fight in defence of their own lives, they may and they must fight in defence of the lives of others: if they may fight in defence of the lives of others, they will fight in defence of their property: if in defence of property, they will fight in defence of political rights: if in defence of rights, they will fight in promotion of interests: if in promotion of interests, they will fight in promotion of their glory and their crimes. Now let any man of honesty look over the gradations by which we arrive at this climax, and I believe he will find that, *in practice*, no curb can be placed upon the conduct of an army until they reach it. There is, indeed, a wide distance between fighting in defence of life and fighting in furtherance of our crimes; but the steps which lead from one to the other will follow in inevitable succession. I know that the letter of our rule excludes it, but I know the rule will be a letter only. It is very easy for us to sit in our studies, and to point the commas, and semicolons, and periods of the soldier's career; it is very easy for us to say he shall stop at defence of life, or at protection of property, or at the support of rights; but armies will never listen to us—we shall be only the Xerxes of morality throwing our idle chains into the tempestuous ocean of slaughter.

What is the testimony of experience? When nations are mutually exasperated, and armies are levied, and battles are fought, does not every one know that with whatever motives of defence one party may have begun the contest, both, in turn, become aggressors? In the fury of slaughter, soldiers do not attend, they cannot attend, to questions of aggression. Their business is destruction, and their business they will perform. If the army of defence obtains success, it soon becomes an army of aggression. Having repelled the invader, it begins to punish him. If a war is once begun, it is vain to think of distinctions of aggression and defence. Moralists may *talk* of distinctions, but soldiers will *make* none; and none can be made; it is without the limits of possibility.

But, indeed, what is defensive war? A celebrated moralist defines it to be, war undertaken in consequence of "*an injury* perpetrated, attempted, or feared;" which shows with sufficient clearness how little *the assassin* concerns the question, for fear respecting life does not enter into the calculation of "injuries." So, then, if we fear some injury to our purses, or to our "honour," we are allowed to send an army to the country that gives us fear, and to slaughter its inhabitants; and this, we are told, is defensive war. By this system of reasoning, which has been happily called "martial logic," there will be little difficulty in proving any war to be defensive. Now we say that if Christianity allows defensive war, she allows all war—except indeed that of simple aggression; and by the rules of this morality, the aggressor is difficult of discovery; for he whom we choose to "fear" may say that he had previous "fear" of us, and that his "fear" prompted the hostile symptoms which made us "fear" again. The truth is, that to attempt to make any distinctions upon the subject is vain. War must be wholly forbidden, or allowed without restriction to defence; for no definitions of lawful or unlawful war will be, or can be, attended to. If the principles of Christianity, in any case, or for any purpose, allow armies to meet and to slaughter one another, her principles will never conduct us to the period which prophecy has assured us they shall produce. There is no hope of an eradication of war but by an absolute and total abandonment of it.*

What then is the principle for which we contend? *An unreasoning reliance upon Providence for defence, in all those cases in which we should violate His laws by defending ourselves.* The principle can claim a species of merit which must at least be denied to some systems of morality—that of simplicity, of easiness of apprehension, of adaptation to every understanding, of applicability to every circumstance of life.

If a wisdom which we acknowledge to be unerring, has determined and declared that any given conduct is right, and that it is good for man, it appears preposterous and irreverent to argue that another can be better. The Almighty certainly *knows* our interests, and if he has not directed us in the path which promotes them, the conclusion is inevitable that he has voluntarily directed us amiss.—Will the advocate of war abide this conclusion? And if he will not, how will he avoid the opposite conclusion, that the path of forbearance is the path of expediency?

* It forms no part of a Christian's business to inquire why his religion forbids any given actions, although I know not that the inquiry is reprehensible. In the case of personal attack, possibly Christianity may decide, that if one of two men must be hurried from the world, of whom the first is so profligate as to assault the life of his fellow, and the other is so virtuous as to prefer the loss of life to the abandonment of Christian principles—it is more consistent with her will that the good should be transferred to his hoped felicity, than that the bad should be consigned to punishment.

It would seem to be a position of very simple truth, that it becomes an *erring* being to regulate his actions by an acquiescent reference to an unerring will. That it is necessary for one of these erring beings formally to insist upon this truth, and systematically to prove it to his fellows, may reasonably be a subject of grief and of shame. But the hardihood of guilt denies the truth, and the speculativeness of philosophy practically supersedes it;—and the necessity therefore remains.

We have seen that the duties of the religion which God has imparted to mankind require irresistance; and surely it is reasonable to believe, even without a reference to experience, that he will make our irresistance subservient to our interests—that if, for the purpose of conforming to his will, we subject ourselves to difficulty or danger, he will protect us in our obedience, and direct it to our benefit—that if he requires us not to be concerned in war, he will preserve us in peace—that he will not desert those who have no other protection, and who have abandoned all other protection because they confide in his alone.

And if we refer to experience, we shall find that the reasonableness of this confidence is confirmed. There have been thousands who have confided in Heaven in opposition to all their apparent interests, but of these thousands has one eventually said that he repented his confidence, or that he reposed in vain?— "He that will lose his life for my sake and the gospel's, the same shall find it." If it be said that we take futurity into the calculation, in our estimate of *interest*, I answer—So we ought. Who is the man that would exclude futurity; or what are his principles? I do not comprehend the foundation of those objections to a reference to futurity which are thus flippantly made. Are we not immortal beings? Have we not interests beyond the present life? It is a deplorable temper of mind which would diminish the frequency, or the influence, of our references to futurity. The prospects of the future *ought* to predominate over the sensations of the present. And if the attainment of this predominance be difficult, let us at least, not voluntarily, argumentatively, persuade ourselves to forego the prospect, or to diminish its influence.

Yet, even in reference only to the present state of existence, I believe we shall find that the testimony of experience is, that forbearance is most conducive to our interests.

> Integer vitæ scelerisque purus
> Non eget Mauri jaculis neque arcu,
> Nec venenatis gravida sagittis,
> Fusce, pharetra.
>
> HORACE.

And the same truth is delivered by much higher authority than that of Horace, and in much stronger language:—"If a man's ways please the Lord, he maketh even his *enemies to be at peace with him.*"

The reader of American history will recollect that in the beginning of the last century, a desultory and most dreadful warfare was carried on by the natives against the European settlers; a warfare that was provoked, as such warfare has almost always originally been, by the injuries and violence of the Christians. The mode of destruction was secret and sudden. The barbarians sometimes lay in wait for those who might come within their reach on the highway or in the fields, and shot them without warning; and sometimes they attacked the Europeans in their houses, "scalping some, and knocking out the brains of others." From this horrible warfare, the inhabitants sought safety by abandoning their homes, and retiring to fortified places, or to the neighborhood of garrisons; and those whom necessity still compelled to pass beyond the limits of such protection, provided themselves with arms for their defence. But amidst this dreadful desolation and universal terror, the *Society of Friends,* who were a considerable proportion of the whole population, were steadfast to their principles. They would neither retire to garrisons, nor provide themselves with arms. They remained openly in the country, whilst the rest were flying to the forts. They still pursued their occupations in the fields or at their homes, without a weapon either for annoyance or defence. And what was their fate? They lived in security and quiet. The habitation, which to his armed neighbor, was the scene of murder and of the scalping knife, was to the unarmed Quaker a place of safety and of peace.

Three of the Society were however killed. And who were they? They were three who abandoned their principles. Two of these victims were men, who, in the simple language of the narrator, "used to go to their labor without any weapons, and trusted to the Almighty, and depended on his providence to protect them (it being their principle not to use weapons of war to offend others or to defend themselves): *but a spirit of distrust* taking place in their minds, they took weapons of war to defend themselves, and the Indians, who had seen them several times without them, and let them alone, saying they were peaceable men and hurt nobody, therefore they would not hurt them,—now seeing them have guns, and supposing they designed to kill the Indians, they therefore shot the men dead." The third whose life was sacrificed was a woman, who " had remained in her habitation," not thinking herself warranted in going " to a fortified place for preservation, neither she, her son, nor daughter, nor to take thither the little ones; but the poor woman after some time began to let in a slavish fear, and advised her children to go with her to a fort not far from their dwelling." She went ;—and shortly afterwards " the bloody, cruel Indians lay by the way, and killed her."*

The fate of the Quakers during the rebellion in Ireland was nearly similar. It is well known that the rebellion was a time not only of open war but of cold-blooded murder; of the utmost fury of bigotry, and the utmost exasperation of revenge. Yet the Quakers were preserved even to a proverb; and when strangers passed through streets of ruin, and observed a house standing uninjured and alone, they would sometimes point and say—" That doubtless, was the house of a Quaker."

It were to no purpose to say, in opposition to the evidence of these facts, that they form an exception to a general rule. The exception to the rule consists in the *trial* of the experiment of non-resistance, not in its *success*. Neither were it to any pur-

---

* See " Select Anecdotes, &c., by John Barclay," pp. 71—79. In this little volume I have found some illustrations of the *policy* of the principle which we maintain in the case of a personal attack. Barclay, the celebrated Apologist, was attacked by a highwayman. He made no other resistance than a calm expostulation. The felon dropped his presented pistol, and offered no farther violence. A Leonard Fell was assaulted by a highway robber, who plundered him of his money and his horse, and afterwards threatened to blow out his brains. Fell solemnly spoke to the robber on the wickedness of his life. The man was astonished :—he declared he would take neither his money nor his horse, and returned them both.—" If thine enemy hunger, feed him,—for in so doing thou shalt heap coals of fire upon his head."

pose to say, that the savages of America or the desperadoes of Ireland spared the Quakers because they were *previously* known to be an unoffending people, or because the Quakers had *previously* gained the love of these by forbearance or good offices:—we concede all this; it is the very argument which we maintain. We say that a *uniform, undeviating* regard to the peaceable obligations of Christianity, *becomes the safeguard of those who practise it.* We venture to maintain that no reason whatever can be assigned why the fate of the Quakers would not be the fate of *all* who should adopt their conduct. No reason can be assigned why, if their number had been multiplied ten-fold or a hundred-fold, they would not have been preserved. If there be such a reason, let us hear it. The American and Irish Quakers were, to the rest of the community, what one nation is to a continent. And we must require the advocate of war to produce (that which has never yet been produced) a reason for believing that, although individuals exposed to destruction were preserved, a nation exposed to destruction would be destroyed. We do not, however, say, that if a people, in the customary state of men's passions, should be assailed by an invader, and should, on a sudden, choose to declare that they would try whether Providence would protect them—of such a people, we do not say that they would experience protection, and that none of them would be killed. But we say that the evidence of experience is, that a people who habitually regard the obligations of Christianity in their conduct towards other men, and who steadfastly refuse, through whatever consequences, to engage in acts of hostility, *will experience protection in their peacefulness:* and it matters nothing to the argument, whether we refer that protection to the immediate agency of Providence, or to the influence of such conduct upon the minds of men.

Such has been the experience of the unoffending and unresisting, in individual life. A *national* example of a refusal to bear arms has only once been exhibited to the world; but that one example has proved, so far as its political circumstances enabled it to prove, all that humanity could desire, and all that skepticism could demand, in favor of our argument.

It has been the ordinary practice of those who have colonized distant countries, to force a footing, or to maintain it, with the sword. One of the first objects has been to build a fort and to provide a military. The adventurers became soldiers, and the colony was a garrison. Pennsylvania was, however, colonized by men who believed that war was absolutely incompatible with Christianity, and who therefore resolved not to practise it. Having determined not to fight, they maintained no soldiers and possessed no arms. They planted themselves in a country that was surrounded by savages, and by savages who knew they were unarmed. If easiness of conquest, or incapability of defence, could subject them to outrage, the Pennsylvanians might have been the very sport of violence. Plunderers might have robbed them without retaliation, and armies might have slaughtered them without resistance. If they did not give a temptation to outrage, no temptation could be given. But these were the people who possessed their country in security, whilst those around them were trembling for their existence. This was a land of peace, whilst every other was a land of war. The conclusion is inevitable, although it is extraordinary—they were in no need of arms *because they would not use them.*

These Indians were sufficiently ready to commit outrages upon other states, and often visited them with desolation and slaughter; with that sort of desolation, and that sort of slaughter, which might be expected from men whom civilization had not reclaimed from cruelty, and whom religion had not awed into forbearance. "But whatever the quarrels of the Pennsylvanian Indians were with others, they uniformly respected, and held as it were sacred, the territories of William Penn."* "The Pennsylvanians never lost man, woman, or child by them, which neither the colony of Maryland, nor that of Virginia could say, no more than the great colony of New England."†

The security and quiet of Pennsylvania was not a transient freedom from war. such as might accidentally happen to any nation. She continued to enjoy it "for more than seventy years,"‡ and subsisted in the midst of six Indian nations, "without so much as a militia for her defence."§ "The Pennsylvanians became armed, though without arms; they became strong, though without strength; they became safe, without the ordinary means of

---

* Clarkson. † Oldmixon, Anno 1708 ‡ Proud. § Oldmixon.

safety. The constable's staff was the only instrument of authority amongst them for the greater part of a century, and never, during the administration of Penn or that of his proper successors, was there a quarrel or a war."*

I cannot wonder that these people were not molested—extraordinary and unexampled as their security was. There is something so noble in this perfect confidence in the Supreme Protector, in this utter exclusion of " slavish fear," in this voluntary relinquishment of the means of injury or of defence, that I do not wonder that even ferocity could be disarmed by such virtue. A people, generously living without arms, amidst nations of warriors! Who would attack a people such as this? There are few men so abandoned as not to respect such confidence. It were a peculiar and an unusual intensity of wickedness that would not even revere it.

And when was the security of Pennsylvania molested, and its peace destroyed?—When the men who had directed its counsels and *who would not engage in war*, were *outvoted in its legislature:* when *they who supposed that there was greater security in the sword than in Christianity*, became the predominating body. From that hour, the Pennsylvanians transferred their confidence in Christian principles to a confidence in their arms; and from that hour to the present they have been subject to war.

Such is the evidence derived from a national example of the consequences of a pursuit of the Christian policy in relation to war. Here are a people who absolutely refused to fight, and who incapacitated themselves for resistance by refusing to possess arms, and this was the people whose land, amidst surrounding broils and slaughter, was selected as a land of security and peace. The only national opportunity which the virtue of the Christian world has afforded us of ascertaining the safety of relying upon God for defence, has determined that it is safe.

If the evidence which we possess do not satisfy us of the expediency of confiding in God, what evidence do we ask, or what can we receive? We have his promise that he will protect those who abandon their seeming interests in the performance of his will, and we have the testimony of those who have confided in

* Clarkson, Life of Penn.

him, that he has protected them. Can the advocate of war produce one single instance in the history of man, of a person who had given an unconditional obedience to the will of heaven, and who did not find that his conduct was *wise* as well as virtuous, that it accorded with his *interests* as well as with his duty? We ask the same question in relation to the peculiar obligations to irresistance. Where is the man who regrets, that in observance of the forbearing duties of Christianity, he consigned his preservation to the superintendence of God?—And the solitary national example that is before us, confirms the testimony of private life; for there is sufficient reason for believing that no nation, in modern ages, has possessed so large a portion of virtue or of happiness as Pennsylvania before it had seen human blood. I would therefore repeat the question—What evidence do we ask, or can we receive?

This is the point from which we wander—WE DO NOT BELIEVE IN THE PROVIDENCE OF GOD. When this statement is formally made to us, we think, perhaps, that it is not true; but our practice is an evidence of its truth—for if we did believe, we should also *confide* in it, and should be willing to stake upon it the consequences of our obedience.* We can talk with sufficient fluency of "trusting in Providence," but in the application of it to our conduct in life, we know wonderfully little. Who is it that confides in Providence, and for what does he trust him? Does his confidence induce him to set aside his own views of interest and safety, and simply to obey precepts which appear inexpedient and unsafe? This is the confidence that is of value, and of which we know so little. There are many who believe that war is disallowed by Christianity, and who would rejoice that it were for ever abolished; but there are few who are willing to maintain an undaunted and unyielding stand against it. They can talk of the loveliness of peace, ay, and argue against the lawfulness of war; but when difficulty or suffering would be the consequence, they will not refuse to do what they know to be unlaw-

---

* "The dread of being destroyed by our enemies if we do not go to war with them, is a plain and unequivocal proof of our disbelief in the superintendence of Divine Providence."—*The Lawfulness of defensive War impartially considered; by a Member of the Church of England.*

ful, they will not practise the peacefulness which they say they admire. Those who are ready to sustain the consequences of undeviating obedience are the supporters of whom Christianity stands in need. She wants men who are willing to *suffer* for her principles.

It is necessary for us to know by what principles we are governed. Are we regulated by the injunctions of God or are we not? If there be any lesson of morality which it is of importance to mankind to learn, and if there be any which they have not yet learnt, it is the necessity of simply performing the duties of Christianity without reference to consequences. If we could persuade ourselves to do this, we should certainly pass life with greater consistency of conduct, and as I firmly believe, in greater enjoyment and greater peace. The world has had many examples of such fidelity and confidence. Who have been the Christian martyrs of all ages, but men who maintained their fidelity to Christianity through whatever consequences? *They* were faithful to the Christian creed; *we* ought to be faithful to the Christian morality; without morality the profession of a creed is vain. Nay, we have seen that there have been martyrs to the duties of morality, and to these very duties of *peacefulness*. The duties remain the same, but where is our obedience?

I hope, for the sake of his understanding and his heart, that the reader will not say I reason on the supposition that the world was what it is not; and that although these duties may be binding upon us when the world shall become purer, yet that we must now accommodate ourselves to the state of things as they are. This is to say that in a land of assassins, assassination would be right. If no one begins to reform his practice, until others have begun before him, reformation will never be begun. If apostles, or martyrs, or reformers had " accommodated themselves to the existing state of things," where had now been Christianity? The business of reformation belongs to him who sees that reformation is required. The world has no other human means of amendment. If you believe that war is not allowed by Christianity, it is your business to oppose it; and if fear or distrust should raise questions on the consequences, apply the words of our Saviour—" What is that to thee?—Follow thou me."

Our great misfortune in the examination of the duties of Christianity, is, that we do not contemplate them with sufficient simplicity. We do not estimate them without some addition or abatement of our own; there is almost always some intervening medium. A sort of half transparent glass is hung before each individual, which possesses endless shades of colour and degrees of opacity, and which presents objects with endless varieties of distortion. This glass is coloured by our education and our passions. The business of moral culture is to render it transparent. The perfection of the perceptive part of moral culture is to remove it from before us.—*Simple obedience without reference to consequences*, is our great duty. I know that philosophers have told us otherwise: I know that we have been referred, for the determination of our duties, to calculations of expediency and of the future consequences of our actions:—but I believe that in whatever degree this philosophy directs us to forbear an unconditional obedience to the rules of our religion, it will be found, that when Christianity shall advance in her purity and her power, she will sweep it from the earth with the besom of destruction.

The positions, then, which we have endeavored to establish, are these:—

I. That the general character of Christianity is wholly incongruous with war, and that its general duties are incompatible with it.
II. That some of the express precepts and declarations of Jesus Christ virtually forbid it.
III. That his practice is not reconcileable with the supposition of its lawfulness.
IV. That the precepts and practice of the apostles correspond with those of our Lord.
V. That the primitive Christians believed that Christ had forbidden war; and that some of them suffered death in affirmance of this belief.
VI. That God has declared in prophecy, that it is his will that war should eventually be eradicated from the earth; and this eradication will be effected by Christianity, by the influence of its *present* principles.
VII. That those who have refused to engage in war, in consequence of their belief of its inconsistency with Christianity, have found that Providence has protected them.

Now we think that the establishment of any considerable number of these positions is sufficient for our argument. The establishment of the whole forms a body of evidence, to which I am not able to believe that an inquirer, to whom the subject was new, would be able to withhold his assent. But since such an inquirer cannot be found, I would invite the reader to lay prepossession aside, to suppose himself to have now first heard of battles and slaughter, and dispassionately to examine whether the evidence in favour of peace be not very great, and whether the objections to it bear any proportion to the evidence itself. But whatever may be the determination upon this question, surely it is reasonable to try the experiment whether security cannot be maintained without slaughter. Whatever be the reasons for war, it is certain that it produces enormous mischief. Even waiving the obligations of Christianity, we have to choose between evils that are certain and evils that are doubtful; between the actual endurance of a great calamity, and the possibility of a less. It certainly cannot be proved that peace would not be the best policy; and since we know that the present system is bad, it were reasonable and wise to try whether the other is not better. In reality, I can scarcely conceive the possibility of greater evil than that which mankind now endure; an evil, moral and physical, of far wider extent, and far greater intensity, than our familiarity with it allows us to suppose. If a system of peace be not productive of less evil than the system of war, its consequences must indeed be enormously bad; and that it would produce such consequences, we have no warrant for believing either from reason or from practice—either from the principles of the moral government of God, or from the experience of mankind. Whenever a people shall pursue, steadily and uniformly, the pacific morality of the gospel, and shall do this from the pure motive of obedience, there is no reason to fear for the consequences: there is no reason to fear that they would experience any evils such as we now endure, or that they would not find that Christianity understands their interests better than themselves; and that the surest and the only rule of wisdom, of safety, and of expediency, is to maintain her spirit in every circumstance of life.

"There is reason to expect," says Dr. Johnson, "that as the world is more enlightened, policy and morality will at last be reconciled."* When this enlightened period shall arrive, we shall be approaching, and we shall not till then approach, that era of purity and of peace, when "violence shall be no more heard in our land, wasting nor destruction within our borders"—that era in which God has promised that "they shall not hurt nor destroy in all his holy mountain." That a period like this will come, I am not able to doubt: I believe it because it is not credible that he will always endure the butchery of man by man; because he has declared that he will not endure it; and because I think there is a perceptible approach of that period in which he will say—"It is enough."† In this belief I rejoice: I rejoice that the number is increasing of those who are asking,—" Shall the sword devour for ever?" and of those who, whatever be the opinions or the practice of others, are openly saying, "I am for peace."‡

Whether I have succeeded in establishing the position THAT WAR, OF EVERY KIND, IS INCOMPATIBLE WITH CHRISTIANITY, it is not my business to determine; but of this, at least, I can assure the reader, that I would not have intruded this inquiry upon the public, if I had not believed, with undoubting confidence, that the position is accordant with everlasting truth;—with that truth which should regulate our conduct here, and which will not be superseded in the world that is to come.

* Falkland's Islands. † 2 Sam. xxiv. 16. ‡ Psalm cxx. 7.

III.

OBSERVATIONS ON THE EFFECTS OF WAR.

War's least horror is th' ensanguin'd field.—Barbauld.

There are few maxims of more unfailing truth than that " A tree is known by its fruits;" and I will acknowledge that if the lawfulness of war were to be determined by a reference to its consequences, I should willingly consign it to this test, in the belief that, if popular impressions were suspended, a good, or a benevolent, or a reasoning man would find little cause to decide in its favour.

In attempting to illustrate some of the effects of war, it is my purpose to inquire not so much into its civil or political, as into its moral consequences; and of the latter, to notice those, chiefly, which commonly obtain little of our inquiry or attention. To speak strictly indeed, civil and political considerations are necessarily involved in the moral tendency: for the happiness of society is always diminished by the diminution of morality; and enlightened policy knows that the greatest support of a state is the virtue of the people.

The reader needs not be reminded of—what nothing but the frequency of the calamity can make him forget—the intense sufferings and irreparable deprivations which a battle inevitably entails upon private life. These are calamities of which the world thinks little, and which, if it thought of them, it could not remove. A father or a husband can seldom be replaced: a void is created in the domestic felicity, which there is little hope that the future will fill. By the slaughter of a war, there are thousands who weep in unpitied and unnoticed secrecy, whom the world does not see; and thousands who retire, in silence, to hopeless poverty, for whom it does not care. To these, the conquest of a kingdom is of little importance. The loss of a protector or a friend is ill repaid by empty glory. An addition of territory may add titles to a king, but the brilliancy of a crown throws little light upon domestic gloom. It is not my intention to insist upon these calamities, intense, and irreparable, and unnumbered as they are; but those who begin a war without taking them into their estimates of its consequences, must be regarded as, at most, half-seeing politicians. The legitimate object of political measures is the good of the people—and a great sum of good a war must produce, if it outbalances even *this* portion of its mischiefs.

In the more obvious effects of war, there is, however, a sufficient sum of evil and wretchedness. The most dreadful of these is the destruction of human life. The frequency with which this destruction is represented to our minds has almost extinguished our perception of its awfulness and horror. In the interval between anno 1141 and 1815, our country has been at war with France alone, *two hundred and sixty-six years*. If to this we add our wars with other countries, probably we shall find that one-half of the last six or seven centuries has been spent by this country in war! A dreadful picture of human violence! There is no means of knowing how many victims have been sacrificed during this lapse of ages. Those who have fallen in battle, and those who have perished "in tents and ships, amidst damps and putrefaction," probably amount to a number greater than the number of men now existing in France and England together. And where is our equivalent good?—"The wars of Europe, for these two hundred years last past, by the confession of all parties, have really ended in the advantage of none, but to the manifest detriment of all." This is the testimony of the celebrated Dr. Josiah Tucker, Dean of Gloucester: and Erasmus has said, "I know not whether ANY war ever succeeded so fortunately in all its events, but that the conqueror, if he had a heart to feel or an understanding to judge as he ought to do, repented that he had ever engaged in it at all."

Since the last war, we have heard much of the distresses of the country; and whatever be the opinion whether they have been brought upon us by the peace, none will question whether they have been brought upon us by war. The peace may be the occasion of them, but war has been the cause. I have no wish to declaim upon the amount of our national debt—that it is a great evil, and that it has been brought upon us by successive contests, no one disputes. Such considerations ought, undoubtedly, to influence the conduct of public men in their disagreements with other states, even if higher considerations do not influence it. They ought to form part of the calculations of the evil of hostility. I believe that a greater mass of human suffering and loss of human enjoyment are occasioned by the pecuniary distresses of a war, than any ordinary advantages of a war compensate. But this consideration seems too remote to obtain our notice. Anger at offence, or hope of triumph, overpowers the sober calculations of reason, and outbalances the weight of after and long continued calamities. If the happiness of the people were, what it ought to be, the primary and the ultimate object of national measures, I think that the policy which pursued this object would often find that even the pecuniary distresses resulting from a war make a greater deduction from the quantum of felicity, than those evils which the war may have been designed to avoid. At least the distress is certain; the advantage doubtful. It is known that during the past eight years of the present peace, a considerable portion of the community have been in suffering in consequence of war. Eight years of suffering to a million of human creatures, is a serious thing! "It is no answer to say, that this universal suffering, and even the desolation that attends it, are the inevitable consequences and events of war, how warrantably soever entered into, but rather an argument that *no war* can be warrantably entered into, that may produce such intolerable mischiefs."*

There is much of truth, as there is of eloquence, in these observations of one of the most acute intellects that our country has produced :—" It is wonderful with what coolness and indifference the greater part of mankind see war commenced. Those that

* Lord Clarendon—who, however, excepts those wars which are likely "to introduce as much benefit to the world, as damage and inconvenience to a part of it." The morality of this celebrated man, also, seems thus to have been wrecked upon the rock of *expediency.*

hear of it at a distance, or read of it in books, but have never presented its evils to their minds, consider it as little more than a splendid game, a proclamation, an army, a battle and a triumph. Some, indeed, must perish in the most successful field; but they *die upon the bed of honor, resign their lives amidst the joys of conquest, and filled with England's glory, smile in death.* The life of a modern soldier is ill represented by heroic fiction. War has means of destruction more formidable than the cannon and the sword. Of the thousands and ten thousands that perished in our late contests with France and Spain, a very small part ever felt the stroke of an enemy. The rest languished in tents and ships, amidst damps and putrefaction, gasping and groaning, unpitied amongst men made obdurate by long continuance of hopeless misery; and were at last whelmed in pits, or heaved into the ocean, without notice and without remembrance. By incommodious encampments and unwholesome stations, where courage is useless and enterprise impracticable, fleets are silently dispeopled, and armies sluggishly melted away.

"Thus is a people gradually exhausted, for the most part with little effect. The wars of civilized nations make very slow changes in the system of empire. The public perceives scarcely any alteration but an increase of debt; and the few individuals who are benefited are not supposed to have the clearest right to their advantages. If he that shared the danger enjoyed the profit, and after bleeding in the battle, grew rich by the victory, he might show his gains without envy. But at the conclusion of a ten years' war, how are we recompensed for the death of multitudes, and the expense of millions, but by contemplating the sudden glories of paymasters and agents, and contractors and commissaries, whose equipages shine like meteors, and whose palaces rise like exhalations?

"These are the men, who without virtue, labor, or hazard, are growing rich as their country is impoverished; they rejoice when obstinacy or ambition adds another year to slaughter and devastation, and laugh from their desks at bravery and science, while they are adding figure to figure, and cipher to cipher, hoping for a new contract from a new armament, and computing the profits of a siege or a tempest."*

* Johnson—Falkland's Islands.

Our business, however, is principally with the moral effects of war.

"The tenderness of nature, and the integrity of manners, which are driven away or powerfully discountenanced by the corruption of war, are not quickly recovered—and the weeds which grow up in the shortest war, can hardly be pulled up and extirpated without a long and unsuspected peace."—" War introduces and propagates opinions and practice as much against heaven as against earth;—it lays our natures and manners as waste as our gardens and our habitations; and we can as easily preserve the beauty of the one as the integrity of the other, under the cursed jurisdiction of drums and trumpets."*

" War does more harm to the morals of men than even to their property and persons."† "It is a temporary repeal of all the principles of virtue."‡ " There is not a virtue of gospel goodness but has its death-blow from war."§

I do not know whether the greater sum of moral evil resulting from war, is suffered by those who are immediately engaged in it, or by the public. The mischief is most extensive upon the community, but upon the profession it is most intense.

<blockquote>Rara fides pietasque viris qui castra sequuntur.
LUCAN.</blockquote>

No one pretends to applaud the morals of an army, and for its religion, few think of it at all. A soldier is depraved even to a proverb. The fact is too notorious to be insisted upon, that thousands who had filled their stations in life with propriety, and been virtuous from principle, have lost, by a military life both the practice and the regard of morality; and when they have become habituated to the vices of war, have laughed at their honest and plodding brethren who are still spiritless enough for virtue, or stupid enough for piety. The vices which once had shocked them, become the subject, not of acquiescence, but of exultation. "Almost all the professions," says Dr. Knox, "have some characteristic manners, which the professors seem to adopt with little

---

* Lord Clarendon's Essays.   † Erasmus.
‡ Hall.   § William Law, A. M.

examination, as necessary and as honorable distinctions. It happens, unfortunately, that profligacy, libertinism, and infidelity are thought, by weaker minds, almost as necessary a part of a soldier's uniform, as his shoulderknot. To hesitate at an oath, to decline intoxication, to profess a regard for religion, would be almost as ignominious as to refuse a challenge."*

It is, however, not necessary to insist upon the immoral influence of war upon the military character, since no one probably will dispute it. Nor is it difficult to discover how the immorality is occasioned. It is obvious that those who are continually engaged in a practice " in which almost all the vices are incorporated," and who promote this practice with individual eagerness, cannot, without the intervention of a miracle, be otherwise than collectively depraved.

If the soldier engages in the destruction of his species, he should at least engage in it with reluctance, and abandon it with joy. The slaughter of his fellow men should be dreadful in execution and in thought. But what is his aversion or reluctance? He feels none—it is not even a subject of seriousness to him. He butchers his fellow candidates for heaven, as a woodman fells a coppice; with as little reluctance and as little regret.

Those who will compute the tendency of this familiarity with human destruction, cannot doubt whether it will be pernicious to the moral character. What is the hope, that he who is familiar with murder, who has himself often perpetrated it, and who exults in the perpetration, will retain undepraved the principles of virtue? His moral feelings are blunted; his moral vision is obscured. We say his *moral vision* is obscured; for we do not think it possible that he should retain even the *perception* of Christian purity. The soldier, again, who plunders the citizen of another nation without remorse or reflection, and bears away the spoils with triumph, will inevitably lose something of his principles of probity. These principles are shaken; an inroad is made upon their integrity, and it is an inroad that makes after inroads the more easy. Mankind do not generally resist the influence of habit. If we rob and shoot those who are " enemies" to-day, we

---

* Essays.—No. 19 Knox justly makes much exception to the applicability of these censures

are in some degree prepared to shoot and rob those who are not enemies to-morrow. The strength of the restraining *moral principle* is impaired. Law may, indeed, still restrain us from violence; but the power and efficiency of principle is diminished. And this alienation of the mind from the practice, the love, and the perception of Christian purity therefore, of necessity extends its influence to the other circumstances of life; and it is *hence* in part, that the general profligacy of armies arises. That which we have not practised in war we are little likely to practise in peace; and there is no hope we shall possess the goodness which we neither *love* nor *perceive*.

Another means by which war becomes pernicious to the moral character of the soldier, is the incapacity which the profession occasions for the sober pursuits of life. " The profession of a soldier," says Dr. Paley, " almost always unfits men for the business of regular occupations." On the question, whether it be better that of three inhabitants of a village, one should be a soldier and two husbandmen, or that all should occasionally become both, he says that from the latter arrangement the country receives three raw militia men and three *idle and profligate peasants*. War cannot be continual. Soldiers must sometimes become citizens; and citizens who are unfit for stated business will be idle; and they who are idle will scarcely be virtuous. A political project, therefore, such as a war, which will eventually pour fifty or a hundred thousand of such men upon the community, must of necessity be an enormous evil to a state. It were an infelicitous defence to say, that soldiers do not become idle until the war is closed, or they leave the army.—To keep men out of idleness by employing them in cutting other men's limbs and bodies, is at least an extraordinary economy; and the profligacy still remains; for unhappily if war keeps soldiers busy, it does not keep them good.

By a peculiar and unhappy coincidence, the moral evil attendant upon the profession is perpetuated by the after system of *half-pay*. We have no concern with this system on political or pecuniary considerations; but it will be obvious that those who return from war, with the principles and habits of war, are little likely to improve either by a life without necessary occupation or express object. By this system, there are thousands of men, in the prime or in the bloom of life, who live without such object or occupation. This would be an evil if it happened to any set of men, but upon men who have been soldiers the evil is peculiarly intense. He whose sense of moral obligation has been impaired by the circumstances of his former life, and whose former life has induced habits of disinclination to regular pursuits, is the man who, above all others, it is unfortunate for the interests of purity should be supported on "half-pay." If war have occasioned "unfitness for regular occupations," he will not pursue them; if it have familiarized him with profligacy, he will be little restrained by virtue. And the consequences of consigning men under such circumstances to society, at a period of life when the mind is busy and restless and the passions are strong, must, of inevitable necessity be bad.—The officer who leaves the army with the income only which the country allows him, often finds sufficient difficulty in maintaining the character of a gentleman. A gentleman however he will be; and he who resolves to appear rich whilst he is poor, who will not increase his fortune by industry, and who has learnt to have few restraints from principle, sometimes easily persuades himself to pursue schemes of but very exceptionable probity. Indeed, by his peculiar law, the " law of honor," honesty is not required.

I do not know whether it be *politic* that he who has held a commission should not be expected to use a ledger or a yard; but since, by thus becoming a "military gentleman," the number is increased of those who regulate their conduct by the law of honour the rule is necessarily pernicious in its effects. When it is considered that this law allows of " profaneness, neglect of public worship and private devotion, cruelty to servants, rigorous treatment of tenants or other dependants, want of charity to the poor, injuries to tradesmen by insolvency or delay of payment, with numberless examples of the same kind;" that it is, " in most instances, favorable to the licentious indulgence of the natural passions;" that it allows of " adultery, drunkenness, prodigality, duelling, and of revenge in the extreme"*—when all this is considered, it is manifestly inevitable, that those who regulate their conduct by

* Dr. Paley.

the maxims of such a law. must become, as a body, reduced to a low station in the scale of morality.*

We insist upon these things *because they are the consequences of war*. We have no concern with "half-pay," or with the "law of honor," but with war, which extends the evil of the one, and creates the evil of the other. Soldiers may be depraved—and part of their depravity is, undoubtedly, their crime, but part also is their misfortune. *The whole evil* is imputable to war; and we say that this evil forms a powerful evidence against it, whether we direct that evidence to the abstract question of its lawfulness or to the practical question of its expediency. *That* can scarcely be lawful which necessarily occasions such enormous depravity. *That* can scarcely be expedient which is so pernicious to virtue, and therefore to the state.

The economy of war requires of every soldier an implicit submission to his superior; and this submission is required of every gradation of rank to that above it. This system may be necessary to hostile operations, but I think it is unquestionably adverse to intellectual and moral excellence.

The very nature of unconditional obedience implies the relinquishment of the use of the reasoning powers. Little more is required of the soldier than that he be obedient and brave. His obedience is that of an animal which is moved by a goad or a bit, without judgment or volition of his own: and his bravery is that of a mastiff, which fights whatever mastiff others put before him.—It is obvious that in such agency, the intellect and the understanding have little part. Now I think that this is important. He who, with whatever motive, resigns the direction of his conduct implicitly to another, surely cannot retain that erectness and independence of mind, that manly consciousness of mental

---

* There is something very unmanly and cowardly in some of the maxims of this law of honor. How unlike the fortitude, the manliness of real courage, are the motives of him who fights a duel! He accepts a challenge, commonly because he is afraid to refuse it. The question with him is, whether he fears more, *a pistol* or *the world's dread frown;* and his conduct is determined by the preponderating influence of one of these objects of fear. If I am told that he probably feels no fear of death; I answer, that if he fears not the death of a duellist, his principles have sunk to that abyss of depravity, whence nothing but the interposition of Omnipotence is likely to reclaim them.

freedom, which is one of the highest privileges of our nature. The rational being becomes reduced in the intellectual scale; an encroachment is made upon the integrity of its independence. God has given us, individually, capacities for the regulation of our individual conduct. To resign its direction, therefore, to the despotism of another, appears to be an unmanly and unjustifiable relinquishment of the privileges which he has granted to us. Referring simply to the conclusions of reason, I think those conclusions would be, that military obedience must be pernicious to the mind. And if we proceed from reasoning to facts, I believe that our conclusions will be confirmed. Is the military character distinguished by intellectual eminence? Is it not distinguished by intellectual inferiority? I speak of course of the *exercise* of intellect, and I believe that if we look around us, we shall find that no class of men, in a parallel rank in society, exercise it less, or less honorably to human nature, than the military profession.* I do not, however, attribute the want of intellectual excellence solely to the implicit submission of a military life. Nor do I say that this want is so much the fault of the soldier, as of the circumstances to which he is subjected. We attribute this evil also to its rightful parent. The resignation of our actions to the direction of a foreign will, is made so familiar to us by war, and is mingled with so many associations which reconcile it, that I am afraid lest the reader should not contemplate it with sufficient abstraction. Let him remember that in *nothing but in war* do we submit to it.

It becomes a subject yet more serious, if military obedience requires the relinquishment of our moral agency,—if it requires us to do, not only what may be opposed to our will, but what is opposed to our consciences. And it does require this; a soldier must obey, how criminal soever the command, and how criminal

---

* This inferiority will probably be found less conspicuous in the private than in his superiors. Employment in different situations, or in foreign countries, and the consequent acquisition of information, often make the private soldier superior in intelligence to laborers and mechanics; a cause of superiority which, of course, does not similarly operate amongst men of education.

We would here beg the reader to bear in his recollection, the limitations which are stated in the preface, respecting the application of any apparent severity in our remarks.

soever he knows it to be. It is certain that of those who compose armies many commit actions which they believe to be wicked, and which they would not commit but for the obligations of a military life. Although a soldier determinately believes that the war is unjust, although he is convinced that his particular part of the service is atrociously criminal, still he must proceed—he must prosecute the purposes of injustice or robbery; he must participate in the guilt, and be himself a robber. When we have sacrificed thus much of principle, what do we retain? If we abandon all use of our perceptions of good and evil, to what purpose has the capacity of perception been given? It were as well to possess no sense of right and wrong, as to prevent ourselves from the pursuit or rejection of them. To abandon some of the most exalted privileges which heaven has granted to mankind, to refuse the acceptance of them, and to throw them back, as it were, upon the Donor, is surely little other than profane. He who *hid* a talent was of old punished for his wickedness: what then is the offence of him who refuses to receive it? Such a resignation of our moral agency is not contended for or tolerated in any one other circumstance of human life. War stands upon this pinnacle of depravity alone. She only, in the supremacy of crime, has told us that she has abolished even the obligation to be virtuous.

To what a situation is a rational and responsible being reduced, who commits actions, good or bad, mischievous or beneficial, at the word of another? I can conceive no greater degradation. It is the lowest, the final abjectness of the moral nature. It is *this* if we abate the glitter of war, and if we add this glitter it is nothing more. Surely the dignity of reason, and the light of revelation and our responsibility to God, should make us pause before we become the voluntary subjects of this monstrous system.

I do not know, indeed, under what circumstances of *responsibility* a man supposes himself to be placed, who thus abandons and violates his own sense of rectitude and of his duties. Either he is responsible for his actions, or he is not, and the question is a serious one to determine. Christianity has certainly never stated any cases in which personal responsibility ceases. If she admits such cases, she has at least not told us so; but she has told us, explicitly and repeatedly, that she does require individual obedience and impose individual responsibility. She has made no exceptions to the imperativeness of her obligations, whether we are required to neglect them or not; and I can discover in her sanctions, no reason to suppose that in her final adjudications she admits the plea, *that another required us to do that which she required us to forbear.*—But it may be feared, it may be *believed*, that how little soever religion will abate of the responsibility of those who obey, she will impose not a little upon those who command. They, at least, are answerable for the enormities of war; unless, indeed, any one shall tell me that responsibility attaches nowhere; that that which would be wickedness in another man, is innocence in a soldier; and that heaven has granted to the directors of war a privileged immunity, by virtue of which crime incurs no guilt, and receives no punishment.

It appears to me that the obedience which war exacts to arbitrary power, possesses more of the character of servility and even of slavery, than we are accustomed to suppose; and as I think this consideration may reasonably affect our feeling of independence, how little soever higher considerations may affect our consciences, I would allow myself in a few sentences upon the subject. I will acknowledge that when I see a company of men in a stated dress, and of a stated color, ranged, rank and file, in the attitude of obedience, turning or walking at the word of another, now changing the position of a limb, and now altering the angle of a foot, I feel humiliation and shame. I feel humiliation and shame when I think of the capacities and the prospects of man, at seeing him thus drilled into obsequiousness and educated into machinery. I do not know whether I shall be charged with indulging in idle sentiment or idler affectation. If I hold unusual language upon the subject, let it be remembered that the subject is itself unusual. I will retract my affectation and sentiment, if the reader will show me any case in life parallel to that to which I have applied it.

No one questions whether military power *be* arbitrary. *That which governs an army,* says Paley, *is* DESPOTISM: and the subjects of despotic power we call slaves. Yet a man may live under an arbitrary prince with only the *liability* to slavery; he may live and die, unmolested in his person and unrestrained in his freedom.

But the despotism of an army is an operative despotism, and a soldier is practically and personally a slave. Submission to arbitrary authority is the business of his life: the will of the despot is his rule of action.

It is vain to urge that if this be slavery, every one who labours for another is a slave; because there is a difference between the subjection of a soldier and that of all other labourers, in which the essence of slavery consists. If I order my servant to do a given action, he is at liberty, if he think the action improper, or if, from any other cause, he choose not to do it, to refuse his obedience. I can discharge him from my service indeed, but I cannot *compel* obedience or *punish* his refusal. The soldier *is* thus punished or compelled. It matters not whether he have entered the service voluntarily or involuntarily: being there, he is required to do what may be, and what in fact, often is, opposed to his will and his judgment. If he refuse obedience, he is dreadfully punished; his flesh is lacerated and torn from his body, and finally, if he persists in his refusal, he may be shot. Neither is he permitted to leave the service. His natural right to go whither he would, of which nothing but his own crimes otherwise deprives him, is denied to him by war. If he attempt to exercise this right, he is pursued as a felon, he is brought back in irons, and is miserably tortured for "desertion." This, therefore, we think is slavery.

I have heard it contended that an apprentice is a slave equally with a soldier; but it appears to be forgotten that an apprentice is consigned to the government of another because he is not able to govern himself. But even were apprenticeship to continue through life, it would serve the objection but little. Neither custom nor law allows a master to require his apprentice to do an immoral action. There is nothing in his authority analogous to that which compels a soldier to do what he is persuaded is wicked or unjust. Neither, again, can a master compel the obedience of an apprentice by the punishments of a soldier. Even if his commands be reasonable, he cannot, for refractoriness, torture him into a swoon, and then revive him with stimulants only to torture him again; still less can he take him to a field and shoot him. And if the command be vicious, he may not punish his disobedience at all.—Bring the despotism that governs an army into the government of the state, and what would Englishmen say? They would say, with one voice, that Englishmen were slaves.

If this view of military subjection fail to affect our pride, we are to attribute the failure to that power of public opinion by which all things seem reconcilable to us; by which situations, that would otherwise be loathsome and revolting, are made not only tolerable but pleasurable. Take away the influence and the gloss of public opinion from the situation of a soldier, and what should we call it? We should call it a state of insufferable degradation; of pitiable slavery. But public opinion, although it may influence notions, cannot alter things. Whatever may be our notion of the soldier's situation, he has indisputably resigned both his moral and his natural liberty to the government of despotic power. He has added to ordinary slavery, the slavery of the conscience; and he is therefore, in a twofold sense, a slave.

If I be asked why I thus complain of the nature of military obedience, I answer, with Dr. Watson, that all "despotism is an offence against natural justice; it is a degradation of the dignity of man, and ought not, on any occasion, to be either practised or submitted to:"—I answer that the obedience of a soldier does, in point of fact, depress the erectness and independence of his mind;—I answer, again, that it is a sacrifice of his moral agency, which impairs and vitiates his principles, and which our religion emphatically condemns; and, finally and principally I answer, that such obedience is not defended or permitted for any other purpose than the prosecution of war, and that it is therefore a powerful evidence against the solitary system that requires it. I do not question the necessity of despotism to war: it is because I know that it *is* necessary that I thus refer to it; for I say that *whatever* makes such despotism and consequent degradation and vice necessary, must itself be bad, and must be utterly incompatible with the principles of Christianity.*

* I would scarcely refer to the monstrous practice of impressing seamen, because there are many who deplore and many who condemn it. Whether this also be necessary to war, I know not:—probably it is necessary; and if it be, I would ask no other evidence against the system that requires it. Such an invasion of the natural rights of man, such a monstrous assumption of arbitrary power, such a violation of every principle of justice, cannot possibly be necessary to any system of which Christianity approves.

Yet I do not know whether, in its effects on the military character, the greatest moral evil of war is to be sought. Upon the community its effects are indeed less apparent, because they who are the secondary subjects of the immoral influence are less intensely affected by it than the immediate agents of its diffusion. But whatever is deficient in the degree of evil, is probably more than compensated by its extent. The influence is like that of a continual and noxious vapour; we neither regard nor perceive it, but it secretly undermines the moral health.

Every one knows that vice is contagious. The depravity of one man has always a tendency to deprave his neighbours; and it therefore requires no unusual acuteness to discover, that the prodigious mass of immorality and crime, which are accumulated by a war, must have a powerful effect in "demoralizing" the public. But there is one circumstance connected with the injurious influence of war, which makes it peculiarly operative and malignant. It is, that we do not hate or fear the influence, and do not fortify ourselves against it. Other vicious influences insinuate themselves into our minds by stealth: but this we receive with open embrace. If a felon exhibits an example of depravity and outrage, we are little likely to be corrupted by it; because we do not love his conduct or approve it. But from whatever cause it happens, the whole system of war is the subject of our complacency or pleasure; and it is *therefore* that its mischief is so immense. If the soldier who is familiarized with slaughter and rejoices in it, loses some of his Christian dispositions, the citizen who, without committing the slaughter, unites in the exultation, loses also some of his. If he who ravages a city and plunders its inhabitants, impairs his principles of probity, he who approves and applauds the outrage, loses also something of his integrity or benevolence. We acknowledge these truths when applied to other cases. It is agreed that a frequency of capital punishments has a tendency to make the people callous, to harden them against human suffering, and to deprave their moral principles. And the same effect will necessarily be produced by war, of which the destruction of life is incomparably greater, and of which our abhorence is incomparably less.—The simple truth is, that we are gratified and delighted with things which are incompatible with Christianity, and that our minds therefore become alienated from its love. Our affections cannot be fully directed to "two masters." If we love and delight in war, we are little likely to love and delight in the dispositions of Christianity.—And the evil is in its own nature of almost universal operation. During a war, a whole people become familiarized with the utmost excesses of enormity—with the utmost intensity of human wickedness—and they rejoice and exult in them; so that there is probably not an individual in a hundred who does not lose something of his Christian principles by a ten years' war.

The effect of the system in preventing the perception, the love, and the *operation* of Christian principles, in the minds of men who know the nature and obligations of them, needs little illustration. We often *see* that Christianity cannot accord with the system, but the conviction does not often operate on our minds. In one of the speeches of Bishop Watson in the House of Lords, there occur these words:—" Would to God, my lords, that the spirit of the Christian religion would exert its influence over the hearts of individuals in their public capacity; then would revenge, avarice, and ambition, which have fattened the earth with the blood of her children, be banished from the counsels of princes, and there would be no more war. The time will come—the prophet hath said it, and I believe it—the time will assuredly come when nation, literally speaking, shall no longer lift up hand against nation. No man will rejoice, my lords, more than I shall, to see the time when peace shall depend on an obedience to the benevolent principles of the gospel."* This is language becoming a Christian. Would it have been believed that this same man voluntarily and studiously added almost one-half to the power of gunpowder, in order that the ball which before would kill but six men, might now kill ten; and that he did this, knowing that this purpose was to spread wider destruction and bloodier slaughter? Above all, would it be believed that he recorded this achievement as an evidence of his sagacity, and that he recorded it in the book which contains the declaration I have quoted?

The same consequences attach to the influence of the soldier's personal character. Whatever that character be, if it arise out of his profession, we seldom regard it with repulsion. We look

---

* Life of Bishop Watson.

upon him as a man whose *honour and spirit* compensate for "venial errors." If he be spirited and gallant, we ask not for his virtue and care not for his profligacy. We look upon the sailor as a brave and noble fellow, who may reasonably be allowed in droll profaneness, and sailorlike debaucheries—debaucheries, which, in the paid-off crew of a man-of-war, seem sometimes to be animated by

> ——the dissoluted Spirit that fell,
> The fleshliest Incubus.

We are, however, much diverted by them. The sailor's cool and clumsy vices are very amusing to us; and so that he amuses us, we are indifferent to his crimes. That some men should be wicked, is bad—that the many should feel complacency in wickedness is, perhaps, worse. We may flatter ourselves with dreams of our own virtue, but that virtue is very questionable—those principles are very unoperative, which permit us to receive pleasure from the contemplation of human depravity, with whatever "honour or spirit" that depravity is connected. Such principles and virtue will oppose, at any rate, little resistance to temptation. An abhorrence of wickedness is more than an outwork of the moral citadel. He that does not hate vice has opened a passage for its entrance.*

I do not think that those who feel an interest in the virtue and the happiness of the world will regard the animosity of party and the restlessness of resentment which are produced by a war, as trifling evils. If anything be opposite to Christianity, it is retaliation and revenge. In the obligation to restrain these dispositions, much of the characteristic placability of Christianity consists. The very essence and spirit of our religion are abhorrent from resentment.—The very essence and spirit of war are promotive of resentment; and what then must be their mutual adverseness? That war excites these passions, needs not be

---

* All sober men allow this to be true in relation to the influence of those *Novels* which decorate a profligate character with objects of attraction. They allow that our complacency with these subjects abates our hatred of the accompanying vices. And the same also is true in relation to war; with the difference, indeed, which is likely to exist between the influence of the vices of fiction and that of the vices of real life.

proved. When a war is in contemplation, or when it has been begun, what are the endeavours of its promoters? They animate us by every artifice of excitement to hatred and animosity. Pamphlets, placards, newspapers, caricatures—every agent is in requisition to irritate us into malignity. Nay, dreadful as it is, the pulpit resounds with declamations to stimulate our too sluggish resentment, and to invite us to blood.—And thus the most unchristianlike of all our passions, the passion which it is most the object of our religion to repress, is excited and fostered. Christianity cannot be flourishing under circumstances like these. The more effectually we are animated to war, the more nearly we extinguish the dispositions of our religion. War and Christianity are like the opposite ends of a balance, of which one is depressed by the elevation of the other.

These are the consequences which make war dreadful to a state. Slaughter and devastation are sufficiently terrible, but their collateral evils are their greatest. It is *the immoral feeling* that war diffuses—it is *the depravation of principle*, which forms the mass of its mischief.

There is one mode of hostility that is allowed and encouraged by war, which appears to be distinguished by peculiar atrocity; I mean privateering. If war could be shown to be necessary or right, I think this, at least, were indefensible. It were surely enough that army slaughtered army, and that fleet destroyed fleet, without arming individual avarice for private plunder, and legalizing robbery because it is not of our countrymen. Who are the victims of this plunder, and what are its effects? Does it produce any mischief to our enemies but the ruin of those who perhaps would gladly have been friends?—of those who are made enemies only by the will of their rulers, and who now conduct their commerce with no other solicitude about the war than how they may escape the rapine which it sanctions? Privateering can scarcely plead even the merit of public mischief in its favour. An empire is little injured by the wretchedness and starvation of a few of its citizens. The robbery may, indeed, be carried to such extent, and such multitudes may be plundered, that the ruin of individuals may impart poverty to a state. But for *this* mischief the privateer can seldom hope: and what is that practice, of which the only topic of defence is the enormity of its mischief!

There is a yet more dreadful consideration:—The privateer is not only a robber, but a murderer. If he cannot otherwise plunder his victim, human life is no obstacle to his rapine. Robbery is his object, and his object he will attain. Nor has he the ordinary excuses of slaughter in his defence. His government does not require it of him: he makes no pretext of patriotism, but robs and murders of his own choice, and simply for gain. The soldier makes a bad apology when he pleads the command of his superior, but the privateer has no command to plead; and with no object but plunder, he deliberately seeks a set of ruffians who are unprincipled enough for robbery and ferocious enough for murder, and sallies with them upon the ocean, like tigers upon a desert, and like tigers prowling for prey.—To talk of Christianity, as permitting these monstrous proceedings, implies deplorable fatuity or more deplorable profaneness. I would, however, hope that he who sends out a privateer has not so little shame as to pretend to conscience or honesty.—If he will be a robber and a murderer, let him at least not be a hypocrite; for it *is* hypocrisy for such men to pretend to religion or morality. He that thus robs the subjects of another country, wants nothing but impunity to make him rob his neighbour: he has no restraint from principle.

I know not how it happens that men make pretensions to Christianity whilst they *sanction* or *promote* such prodigious wickedness. It is sufficiently certain, that whatever be their pretensions to it, it is not operative upon their conduct. Such men may talk of religion, but they neither possess nor regard it: and although I would not embrace in such censure those who, without immediate or remote participation in the crime, look upon it with secret approbation because it injures their "enemies," I would nevertheless suggest to their consideration whether *their* moral principles are at that point in the scale of purity and benevolence which religion enjoins.

We often hear, during a war, of subsidies from one nation to another for the loan of an army; and we hear of this without any emotion, except perhaps of joy at the greater probability of triumph, or of anger that our money is expended. Yet, surely, if we contemplate such a bargain for a moment, we shall perceive that our first and greatest emotion ought to be abhorrence.—To borrow ten thousand men who know nothing of our quarrel, and care nothing for it, to help us to slaughter their fellows! To pay for their help in guineas to their sovereign! Well has it been exclaimed,

> War is a game, that were their subjects wise,
> Kings would not play at.

A king sells his subjects as a farmer sells his cattle; and sends them to destroy a people, whom, if they had been higher bidders, he would perhaps have sent them to defend. That kings should do this may grieve, but it cannot surprise us: avarice has been as unprincipled in humbler life; the possible malignity of individual wickedness is perhaps without any limit. But that a large number of persons, with the feelings and reason of men, should coolly listen to the bargain of their sale, should compute the guineas that will pay for their blood, and should then quietly be led to a place where they are to kill people towards whom they have no animosity, is simply wonderful. To what has inveteracy of habit reconciled mankind! I have no capacity of supposing a case of slavery, if slavery be denied in this. Men have been sold in another continent, and England has been shocked and aroused to interference; yet these men were sold, not to be slaughtered, but to work: but of the purchases and sales of the world's political butchers, England cares nothing and thinks nothing; nay, she is a participator in the bargains. There is no reason to doubt that upon other subjects of horror, similar familiarity of habit would produce similar effects; or that he who heedlessly contemplates the purchase of an army, wants nothing but this familiarity to make him heedlessly look on at the commission of parricide. If we could for one moment emancipate ourselves from this power of habit, how would it change the scene that is before us! Little would remain to war of splendour or glory, but we should be left with one wide waste of iniquity and wretchedness.

It is the custom, during the continuance of a war, to offer public prayers for the success of our arms; and our enemies pray also for the success of theirs. I will acknowledge that this practice appears to me to be eminently shocking and profane. The idea of two communities of Christians, separated perhaps by a creek, at the same moment begging their common Father to assist them in reciprocal destruction, is an idea of horror to which I know no parallel. *Lord, assist us to slaughter our enemies.* This is our petition.—"Father, forgive them; they know not what they do." This is the petition of Christ.

It is certain that of two contending communities, both cannot be in the right. Yet both appeal to Heaven to avouch the justice of their cause, and both mingle with their petitions for the increase, perhaps, of Christian dispositions, importunities to the God of mercy to assist them in the destruction of one another. Taking into account the ferocity of the request—the solemnity of its circumstances—the falsehood of its representations—the fact that both parties are Christians, and that their importunities are simultaneous to their common Lord, I do not think that the world exhibits another example of such irreverent and shocking iniquity. Surely it were enough that we slaughter one another alone in our pigmy quarrels, without soliciting the Father of the universe to be concerned in them: surely it were enough that each reviles the other with the iniquity of his cause, without each assuring Heaven that *he* only is in the right—an assurance that is false, probably in both, and certainly in one.

To attempt to pursue the consequences of war through all her ramifications of evil were, however, both endless and vain. It is a moral gangrene which diffuses its humours through the whole political and social system. To expose its mischief is to exhibit all evil; for there is no evil which it does not occasion, and it has much that is peculiar to itself.

That, together with its multiplied evils, war produces some good, I have no wish to deny. I know that it sometimes elicits valuable qualities which had otherwise been concealed, and that it often produces collateral and adventitious, and sometimes immediate advantages. If all this could be denied, it would be needless to deny it, for it is of no consequence to the question whether it be proved. That any wide extended system should not produce *some* benefits, can never happen. In such a system, it were an unheard-of purity of evil, which was evil without any mixture of good. But, to compare the ascertained advantages of war, with its ascertained mischiefs, or with the ascertained advantages of a system of peace, and to maintain a question as to the preponderance of good, implies not ignorance, but guilt—not incapacity of determination, but voluntary falsehood.

But I rejoice in the conviction that the hour is approaching, when Christians shall cease to be the murderers of one another. Christian light is certainly spreading, and there is scarcely a country in Europe, in which the arguments for unconditional peace have not recently produced conviction. This conviction is extending in our own country, in such a degree, and upon such minds, that it makes the charge of enthusiasm or folly, vain and idle. The friends of peace, if we choose to despise their opinions, cannot themselves be despised; and every year is adding to their number, and to the sum of their learning and their intellect.

It will perhaps be asked, what then are the duties of a subject who believes that all war is incompatible with his religion, but whose governors engage in a war and demand his service? We answer explicitly, *It is his duty, mildly and temperately, yet firmly, to refuse to serve.*—There are some persons, who, without any determinate process of reasoning, appear to conclude that responsibility for national measures attaches solely to those who direct them; that it is the business of *governments* to consider what is good for the community, and that, in these cases, the duty of the subject is merged in the will of the sovereign. Considerations like these are, I believe, often voluntarily permitted to become opiates of the conscience. *I have no part,* it is said, *in the counsels of the government, and am not therefore responsible for its crimes.* We are, indeed, not responsible for the crimes of our rulers, but we are responsible for our own; and the crimes of our rulers *are* our own; if whilst we believe them to be crimes, we promote them by our co-operation. "It is at all times," says Gisborne, "the duty of an Englishman steadfastly to decline obeying any orders of his superiors, which his conscience should tell him, were in any degree impious or unjust."*
The apostles, who instructed their converts to be subject to every

---

* Duties of Men in Society.

ordinance of man for conscience' sake, and to submit themselves to those who were in authority, and who taught them, that whoever resisted the power, resisted the ordinance of God, made one necessary and uniform provision—*that the magistrate did not command them to do what God had commanded them to forbear.* With the regulations which the government of a country thought fit to establish, the apostles complied, whatever they might think of their wisdom or expediency, provided, and only provided, they did not, by this compliance, abandon their allegiance to the Governor of the world. It is scarcely necessary to observe in how many cases they refused to obey the commands of the governments under which they were placed, or how openly they maintained the duty of refusal, whenever these commands interfered with their higher obligations. It is narrated very early in "the Acts," that one of their number was imprisoned for preaching, that he was commanded to preach no more, and was then released. Soon afterwards all the apostles were imprisoned. " Did we not straitly command you," said the rulers, " that ye should not teach in this name ?" The answer which they made is in point :—" We ought to obey God rather than men."* And this system they continued to pursue. If Cæsar had ordered one of the apostles to be enrolled in his legions, does any one believe that he would have served ?

But those who suppose that obedience in all things is required, or that responsibility in political affairs is transferred from the subject to the sovereign, reduce themselves to a great dilemma. It is to say that we must resign our conduct and our consciences to the will of others, and act wickedly or well, as their good or evil may preponderate, without merit for virtue, or responsibility for crime. If the government direct you to fire your neighbour's property, or to throw him over a precipice, will you obey? If you will not, there is an end of the argument, for if you may reject its authority in one instance, where is the limit to rejection? There is no rational limit but that which is assigned by Christianity, and that is both rational and practicable. If any one should ask the meaning of the words, " Whoso resisteth the power resisteth the ordinance of God"—

---

* Acts vi. 28.

we answer, that it refers to *active* resistance ; *passive* resistance, or non-compliance, the apostles themselves practised. On this point we should be distinctly understood. We are not so inconsistent as to recommend a civil war, in order to avoid a foreign one. *Refusal to obey* is the *final* duty of Christians.

We think, then, that it is the business of every man, who believes that war is inconsistent with our religion, respectfully, but steadfastly, to refuse to engage in it. Let such as these remember that an honorable and an awful duty is laid upon them. It is upon their fidelity, so far as human agency is concerned, that the cause of peace is suspended. Let them then be willing to avow their opinions and to defend them. Neither let them be contented with words, if more than words, if suffering also is required. It is only by the unyielding perseverance of good that corruption can be extirpated. If you believe that Jesus Christ has prohibited slaughter, let not the opinion or the commands of a world induce you to join in it. By this "steady and determinate pursuit of virtue," the benediction which attaches to those who hear the sayings of God and do them, will rest upon you, and the time will come when even the world will honour you, as contributors to the work of human reformation.

www.ingramcontent.com/pod-product-compliance
Lightning Source LLC
Chambersburg PA
CBHW021940160426
43195CB00011B/1172